Medieval Women

T0139469

The end of the hunt

Medieval Women

EILEEN POWER

edited by M. M. POSTAN

CAMBRIDGE
UNIVERSITY PRESS

Shaftesbury Road, Cambridge CB2 8EA, United Kingdom

One Liberty Plaza, 20th Floor, New York, NY 10006, USA

477 Williamstown Road, Port Melbourne, VIC 3207, Australia

314–321, 3rd Floor, Plot 3, Splendor Forum, Jasola District Centre,
New Delhi – 110025, India

103 Penang Road, #05–06/07, Visioncrest Commercial, Singapore 238467

Cambridge University Press is part of Cambridge University Press & Assessment,
a department of the University of Cambridge.

We share the University's mission to contribute to society through the pursuit of
education, learning and research at the highest international levels of excellence.

www.cambridge.org
Information on this title: www.cambridge.org/9781107650152

Medieval Women © Cambridge University Press & Assessment 1975
foreword by Maxine Berg © Cambridge University Press & Assessment 1996

Library of Congress catalogue number: 75-7212

First published 1975
Canto edition first published 1997 (version 5, November 2022)

ISBN 978-1-107-65015-2 Paperback

Contents

Foreword: Eileen Power, 1889–1940

by

Maxine Berg

When G. M. Trevelyan published his *English Social History* in 1944 he dedicated it to the memory of Eileen Power, Economic and Social Historian. Her story has not been told, yet she brought together high academic honours, an international reputation, and a popular literary following in ways the great male historians did not achieve. For Eileen Power, as part of the academic elite, sought to write the history of the broad spectrum of society, and to take this history out beyond the small world of academic audiences. She brought medieval history into the general culture and made social history a prominent part of the historical disciplines. In doing so she was also a leader in the field, staking out new historical subjects and methods.

Eileen Power was educated in Cambridge and taught there for eight years. She subsequently taught at the London School of Economics for the rest of her career. She remained, however, closely connected to Cambridge through friends and other historians, especially J. H. Clapham and his family and M. G. Jones, and she returned there to work most summers over her life.[1] She turned down the almost certain opportunity to hold the Chair of Economic History in Cambridge in 1938 so that her new husband, M. M. Postan, could apply. She finally spent the last two years of her life there as his wife and as a member of the London School of Economics during the war years when it was evacuated to Peterhouse.

Eileen Power was born into a substantial middle-class family in Altrincham, an exclusive suburb of Manchester. She was the oldest of three sisters. Her father had Irish roots; her mother's family was middle class, and there were close connections with two spinster aunts and her maternal grandfather. This extended family was to be important, for her father was convicted of a massive fraud on the Manchester Stock exchange in 1891, was declared a bankrupt in 1893, and served a five-year prison term, and several others in the years afterwards for subsequent financial crime.[2] Her mother moved with her and her baby sisters to Bournemouth and lived for a time under an assumed name. The family was deeply affected by the scandal; they were financially ruined, and given no support by their father's side of the family. Their mother's family was not well off, but provided what support they could. The scandal also had a deep emotional impact on Eileen; she never saw her father again, and perceived his crime as a dark shadow on her life.

Her mother died of consumption when Eileen was 14. The sisters were then brought up by their spinster aunts and maternal grandfather, moving to Oxford to attend the Oxford High School for Girls, the school their mother had wanted them to attend. The school was a part of the Public Day School Trust, with minimal fees and a high academic reputation. There the sisters were brought up to expect that they would earn their living. All went on to university. The school also fostered in Eileen a deep interest in literature and history, and from her school-days she built up a wide-ranging command of poetry and an ability to write it herself.

Eileen Power went to Girton College, Cambridge, in 1907 on a Clothworkers' Scholarship, and also held the Pioneer's Prize for History during the three years she was there. She took a First in both parts of the Historical Tripos in 1910. There was only one other woman in her year among the history students with these results. She was taught history there by Ellen McArthur, an economic historian, and later by Winifred Mercier, who became better known later as an educational-ist.[3] The College, and especially Ellen McArthur, had a close connection with Archdeacon William Cunningham, a Fellow of Trinity and one of the first aca-demic economic historians in England. It was through this connection that Eileen Power was later to follow the path from Girton to the LSE taken before her by Lilian Knowles.

She was also taught by tutors outside the College, though there is now little evi-dence of who these were. She kept an undergraduate essay set by one tutor on the pedestrian question, 'Describe the chief forces at work which made for change in Europe towards the end of the fifteenth century'. His comments on her essay: 'You show a tendency to deal in the a priori imaginative reconstruction which . . . is somewhat dangerous today.'[4] Eileen's comment back was: 'My good man, how else do you expect me to treat the Renaissance?'

Though the Girton history dons played an important part in Eileen's early career, it is unlikely that they filled the role of mentors in her historical interests. Eileen Power was trained in economic history while an undergraduate, but Ellen McArthur was teaching at Girton only for Eileen's first year. Probably a greater influence on her historical interests was provided by Edward Armstrong (1846–1928), Bursar and history tutor at Queen's College, Oxford. Eileen visited him frequently in Oxford during holidays, and his own interests in the Renaissance, languages and travel attracted her. He offered historical advice, lent her books, and asked her out to plays at Bradfield, where he was Warden.[5] He played the older man, mentor and father figure she longed for at an impressionable age.

During Eileen Power's time at Girton the Mistress was Emily E. C. Jones, famous for the high quality of her final examinations, especially in economics. Her success had challenged the position taken by Alfred Marshall, who had fought the participation of women in teaching and in the wider university life of Cambridge. He conceded after Jones's Tripos that women were good at examinations, but this, he argued, was because they were naturally diligent, and they lacked the ability to go further. Jones in fact later published several major treatises on logic.[6] Miss Jones was known as 'Jonah' to the undergraduates, and was later described by Dora Russell, another old Girtonian, as 'fragile and exceedingly ladylike'.[7] The Vice-Mistress was Katherine Jex-Blake, a classics don. She was seen by the students as a severe character, 'thoroughly robust and rather like a horse', and popularly known as 'Kits'.[8]

There was then a marked difference between the older and younger generation of dons. The older ones belonged to or identified with the pioneers of women's higher education; they were Victorian in dress and hairstyle, feminist and committed to the campaign for women's suffrage, and single-mindedly academic. The younger generation was closer to the students who now looked on their education as part of, not an alternative to, futures which might include marriage and family life. Dances, clothes and love affairs were for them as much a part of university life as they had not been for their elders. Eileen joked about Miss Jex-Blake to her friend Margery Garrett in 1910, 'Miss Jex-Blake's latest: "What *is* a camisole?"'[9]

Eileen may not have found the serious bluestocking feminism of the Girton dons particularly appealing, but she certainly became closely involved in feminist and suffragist activities while she was at Girton. Her best friends included Margery Garrett, later Spring-Rice, the niece of Elizabeth Garrett Anderson and Millicent Fawcett and Karin Costelloe, sister of Ray Strachey, daughter of Mary Berenson and niece of Alys Russell. Her other close friend at Girton, and the one with whom she remained in closest touch throughout her life, was Mary Gwladys Jones. She was influenced in her own personal approach to feminism to a large extent by her upbringing in a family of self-reliant women, and by her contemporaries at Girton, but she always maintained a great affection for McArthur and Mercier, who were not only tutors, but leading suffragists of their older generation. She joined the National Union of Women's Suffrage Societies, and was initiated into speaking on platforms by Alys Russell. She later did some organising work for the National Union, and her sister Beryl and several of her close friends became full-time organisers.

This did not divert her from the hard work of preparing for her examinations, and doing enough work in economic history to be hired while still in her final year to coach Newnham students in the subject: 'a great "honnah" for EEP to say nothing of some £25 per annum in her pocket – 18 freshers to coach, and I get 2/6 per paper and 1/6 per hour's coaching once a fortnight'.[10] The First she earned in the Historical Tripos also brought with it the Gilchrist Scholarship.

This took Eileen Power to the Ecole des Chartes in Paris for a year, and there she studied under the supervision of C. V. Langlois, the eminent medieval literary and social historian who also taught Marc Bloch. The time allowed her to range widely over medieval and Renaissance art and literature. She wrote in the autumn of 1910:

> I don't believe one can ever do good work on the history of a period without getting soaked in its literature, art and general atmosphere, and that is what I am doing now . . . I love being able to spread myself over what at college had to be irrelevancies – the art and literature and to feel that duty and pleasure coincide.[11]

She also worked seriously on palaeography, and benefited from Langlois's expertise in that area. At Langlois's suggestion she started a thesis there on Isabella of France, wife of Edward II (popularly known as the 'she-wolf'), and described by Eileen Power as 'the most disreputable woman of her day – her young life was a perfect hotch potch of lovers and murders and plots'.[12]

In the summer of 1911 she returned to England, her funds depleted, and expected to seek a teaching position in a school or a college. She was very unhappy at the prospect of teaching, but knew she had to support herself, and for a time her sisters too. She had written to Margery Garrett from Paris,

> You don't know how I long to be able to research & write books all the time. I am so infinitely more cut out for that than for stumbling along the dull path of dondom, & I could weep sometimes when I think that sooner or later I shall have to start earning my living & only be able to get in fitful research work, in odd moments . . . I'm dead keen on work at present & I will not hurry Isabella & do her badly . . . O Margie, I don't really think I feel like a don. I want to write books. Oh dear, Oh dear![13]

She then heard about a Fellowship at the LSE; she applied for and was awarded the Shaw Research Fellowship there for two years. This paid her £105 a year, and she also assisted Hubert Hall in his research. On this she kept a set of rooms big enough to accommodate her sisters, Rhoda and Beryl, both now at university, during their vacations. Money was always short in the family; the house in Oxford had been given up after her grandfather's death, and one of her aunts was doing secretarial work in London.

Under the terms of her Fellowship, she had to give up her research on Isabella in favour of broader work on medieval women. The LSE did not initially appear very attractive, and she wrote of her feelings:

> I am extremely perturbed because the whole thing has turned out very much more economic than I expected, and I sometimes have doubts whether I am doing the wisest thing . . . I am bound to enter my name for the degree of D.Sc. (Econ) at London. I don't want that degree: I simply detest Economics and always have, and besides I'm a perfect fool at them – the literary and purely historic side is my line.[14]

She was also horrified when the School sent her a list of 'six perfectly disgusting and exclusively narrow economic subjects' to choose from. The topics made her 'weep with boredom'.[15] Despite the topics set her, she did manage a compromise, and pursued research then on medieval English nunneries under the supervision of Hubert Hall at the LSE and G. G. Coulton in Cambridge. The first four chapters were submitted for a London MA, and Power eventually published her first major book on this work, *Medieval English Nunneries*, in 1922.[16]

As it happened, however, Eileen stayed at the LSE for only two years; by the summer of 1912 she was also back tutoring at Girton. After the constant worries over money while she was in London, she now had free rooms and meals in college, and earned £27 6s over the summer. Despite the rapid descent of 'dondom', she was clearly pleased to be back, and was teased by the dons about her clothes.[17] Over the next two years she combined a Directorship of History at Girton with some lectures at the LSE, and lived between Girton and a flat in London she shared with Karen Costelloe. The flat also provided a place during the vacations for her sisters, her friends and the occasional hunger striker or refugee. She felt particularly responsible for Rhoda: 'her delicacy makes her a great responsibility & as I upheld giving up the Oxford house & am moreover the only monied woman (lord!) of the three, the family looks to me to see after her, naturally'.[18] In the spring of 1915 she applied for and got the Pfeiffer Fellowship at Girton with the backing of Lilian Knowles, but continued to do some teaching at the LSE. The Pfeiffer allowed for a reduction of her tutorial teaching, and gave her more opportunity for writing. In 1917 she was awarded the Gamble Prize for an essay, 'The Enclosure Movement in English Nunneries'.[19]

Eileen Power's closest mentor for her research while she was in Cambridge was

G. G. Coulton of St John's. He was the renowned anti-clerical historian of monastic life, with a mission in life to dispel the myth of medieval golden ages in religious life and in the lives of the peasantry. In doing this he wrote not of their ideas or of the laws and customs affecting them, but of their daily lives, with all their peccadilloes and inadequacies. Eileen Power followed Coulton's approach, though with a less polemical tone and more sympathy and wit, applying it to the lives of medieval nuns. The Master's thesis and the book which emerged from it were the first social and economic studies of women's religious communities in the Middle Ages. It broke free of earlier historical traditions in manorial history and medieval religious thought to present a highly readable account of the distribution of wealth among convents, their economic activities and division of labour, and the social backgrounds, daily lives and careers of the nuns. She wrote of her subjects with warmer sympathy than did Coulton of his, for he was much more preoccupied with discrediting the Roman Catholic historians' ideas of the Middle Ages.

Eileen Power also wrote during these years her widely read articles, 'Medieval Ideas about Women', and 'The Position of Women' in Crump and Jacob's *The Legacy of the Middle Ages*. She was dismissive of the latter piece as 'one of those gossips about social life which ought to be bought by the yard at a department store'. Her piece on medieval ideas had originally been rejected by the editors because it was 'not sufficiently respectful of women, the church and the proprieties'.[20] Eileen Power's book and articles, researched and written during these years in Cambridge, established her as an authority on medieval monastic life.[21] When she turned her attention to bourgeois and working women she seemed to enjoy their company more than she had the nuns'.[22] But the novelty of this work, and her ability to comment on women's position across the social spectrum of medieval society reinforced her reputation as a social historian and established her as one of the first major historians of medieval women.

Teaching during these years was dominated by the war and suffrage work. Wartime Cambridge had the reputation of a bleak place of women and old men. But it also opened up some opportunities for women tutors in the University. In practical terms, the early days of the war meant only some disruption to teaching and the presence of soldiers about the place. The war disrupted classes, and by late September 1914 Eileen heard that nearly all the young men at the LSE had enlisted. She wrote to Beveridge offering to postpone her lectures: 'After all it would be horrid to come up weekly for an audience of two or three.'[23] Eileen wrote to Margery in January 1915:

We are having what the Daily News calls Cambridge in the Grip of War. The

War Office at one blow struck our light out and our bells silent on the eve of his Imperial Majesty's birthday . . . And there is a picket of soldiers at the bottom of Woodlands & a barricade of carts & a sentry across Huntingdon Rd & any cars going in & out are stopped & searched & the name of the occupant taken. The Director of Studies in History much enjoys being saluted & questioned by romantic young officers on her way back from her Thursday lecture.[24]

But a few months later the killing had affected her own family, and her youngest uncle had died in Egypt.[25]

Eileen found life in Cambridge very tedious by the later stages of the war, and complained after visiting Margery:

I get the most ghastly blues over the contrast between you & this. I don't believe I was ever cut out for this sort of life: I die within month by month . . . the war makes it worse, for Cambridge is an awful place to be in just now – no one under forty! . . . It seems such a short life for all the best years of it to be spent here . . . I really think the deadliness is chiefly due to abnormal war conditions – there *isn't* anyone to talk to even in Cambridge.

By 1918 she was entertaining hopes of a job coming up eventually in London, and in the meantime, wished that she could go half time at Girton, and have the rest of the week in London.[26]

She survived the time, however, by frequent trips to London, doing some work for the National Union, and doing some lecturing for the WEA and the League of Nations. She gave one with Mrs Fawcett in 1915 at a suffrage meeting, and spoke on the Congress of Vienna,[27] and followed the topic up a few years later for the WEA:

I'll do something I'm very keen on & have just lectured on here – to wit the Congress of Vienna & the attempt at government by a confederation of Europe 1815–23. The parallel with the present is simply amazing . . . it is exceedingly important as propaganda because it broke down for reasons which will wreck the League of Nations after the Congress at the end of this war, if its mistakes aren't avoided.[28]

Eileen was also sustained by her friends among the younger tutors at Girton, especially Elizabeth Downs and M. G. Beard, the German tutor, and by teaching. When Dora Russell was a student she often saw Barbula Beard and Eileen together, Beard 'a tall elegant Irish woman with a slight stoop and a lorgnette and a very agreeable brogue' and Eileen: 'we always found it a pleasure to watch her, tall and placid and very much a personality, as she came in to take her place for dinner at high table. She had very beautiful candid blue-grey eyes.'[29]

Eileen's youth made her a popular and favoured tutor and chaperone, and she was well aware of this:

> I wish it made no difference to the students to have people like me & Pico [Elizabeth Downs] here. And yet when I look at some of them after I've put three years of my best effort – moral & intellectual – into them I cannot conceal from myself that they've started life better equipped than they would have been without us.[30]

Her students, especially the favoured inner circle, clearly idolised her. She was a good lecturer, bringing all into her confidence, and she provided the style, intelligence and wit they all aspired to. She was their 'princess out of a medieval story book' who 'sat at the edge of her chair, offering chocolates'.[31] She had a room with a black carpet and ran poetry and musical evenings, reading avant-garde poets like Rupert Brooke, Ralph Hodgson and W. H. Davies.

Eileen's Sunday poetry readings were an institution: 'We looked forward to them all week and wore our best white or pink crepe de chine blouses in honour of the occasion.'[32] Mary and Theodora Llewelyn Davies, students at Girton between 1914 and 1920 wrote: 'we were a generation of young women starved at a sensitive age of most of the normal poetry of life. Our imaginations were caught and our affections held by Eileen's dazzling personality, by her brilliance, her beauty and her goodness.'[33] The students found themselves somewhat in awe of an intellectual superiority and a social poise that kept them at a distance. Interspersed with these performances, however, were more down-to-earth confessions to Margery Garrett: 'I am feeling dreadfully depressed owing to dowdiness. My new coat & skirt which I got at the end of the summer (a silly thing to do anyhow) looks hopeless and I cannot see in the whole of London a hat that looks decent. Also I want a coat dress more than words can say.'[34]

The war ended, and with it the old enclosed order of the College. The men returned to the University, and Dora Russell was a Fellow in Girton on the occasion when

> just after the First World War ended a horde of undergraduates stormed out from Cambridge, . . . yelling 'where are the women we have been fighting for?' Hanging out of every window and preparing to descend were, needless to say, the women in question. Miss Jex-Blake, like an abbess, in her plain alpaca bodice and full long skirt, followed by a retinue of senior dons, received the invaders at

the doorway under the arch . . . Then she invited them to a dance at the College on the following Saturday. Such a function would not have been thought of only a few years previously.[35]

Dances at Girton were one thing, but integration into the Cambridge academic community was still some way off for the women. Eileen was clearly unhappy with the new 'double standards' of post-war University life. When she was asked to write a women's column for *The Old Cambridge*, she used the space to denounce the idea.

> Let the women of Cambridge speak out in 'The Old Cambridge', but let it be side by side with the men under any of the headings which interest them, and not snugly tucked into their own column, cheek by jowl with the fashions . . . Editors and reviewers are all the same: they think they know a woman's work when they see it . . . But they have no real criterion, because there is no real difference. The difference is between good books and bad books, straight-thinking books and sentimental books, not between male books and female books.[36]

If Cambridge had not yet moved on enough even after the war to accept fully an academic woman like Eileen Power, her own life and those of her friends had. Eileen continued work on her *Nunneries* book, and spent part of the winter and summer of 1917 and 1918 in Coggeshall living in the Paycocke house while she worked on papers there for her *Paycockes of Coggeshall* (1920).[37] She supported Margery Garrett over these years in her pregnancies, the death of a child, and the death of her husband Edward Jones at the Somme. She watched her friends Ruth Dalton, Mary Brinton Stocks and Karin Costelloe Stephen marry,[38] but had herself formed no serious liaisons. The great event of her life was to come with an interview in 1920 for the Kahn Travelling Fellowship.

The Kahn Fellowship was a special prize fellowship providing funding for a year's travel around the world. It had been held in 1912 by Goldsworthy Lowes Dickinson, who used it to travel with E. M. Forster, but it had never before been held by a woman. Eileen Power wrote of her interview with Sir Cooper Perry, the Vice-Chancellor of London University:

> But I rather doubt their giving it to a woman. Sir Cooper Perry obviously did not take women's work very seriously (or perhaps it was me he didn't take seriously!) One of his obiter dicta was 'I have often been amused by women historians; so many of the springs of human action must be hidden from them.' He also suggested that I might defeat the objects of the trust (*sic*) by subsequently committing matrimony, so I suppose he keeps his wife in purdah: anyhow these

silly remarks would not be made to male candidates. However he obviously can't help being made like that, so I possessed my soul in patience and without argument.[39]

This trip, at a still formative part of her life, had a major impact on her subsequent historical interests. Her innovative perspectives on writing comparative social and economic history were first formulated during this year, as were her interests in medieval travellers and merchants. And it was on this trip that she acquired the special attachment to China for which she became well known. While she was in China she met Reginald Johnston, the tutor to the young Emperor of China; on a subsequent trip in 1929 she became engaged to him for a time.

She visited Oscar Browning in Rome, the 'great old boy of Eton and Kings, hero of a hundred stories'. He was then at the age of 83 writing 1,000 words a day of a *History of the World*. In India she joined in debate over reform in the wake of the Amritsar Massacre, attended the Nagpur Congress, and met Gandhi. She found parts of India for 'all the world like the middle ages', something of a relief from the Congress, 'westernised Indians discontented with westernisation'.[40] She spent two months in China, and was profoundly affected by it. She wrote several imaginative pieces and poetry while she was there, and felt herself entering a medieval world. The country touched the romanticised orientalism deeply embedded in her cultural heritage. She was fascinated by its combination of a rationalistic rather than religious outlook with a 'medieval carelessness of all that we mean by progress'.[41] She was to write to Coulton some years afterwards: 'The A.K. fellowship has been my ruin, for my heart will stray outside its clime & period. I think I shall have to compromise by working at the trade between Europe and the East in the middle ages.'[42]

Eileen Power's life was changed even more significantly while she was in China on the Kahn Fellowship journey, for it was there that she received a letter from William Beveridge offering her a job at the London School of Economics. She felt some regrets about leaving friends at Girton, but she was ready to go, her resolve steeled by the vote in Cambridge against giving women University degrees and making them full members of the University. 'I want to be in London for a bit & I'm tired of community life . . . I'm damned tired of being played fast & loose with by Cambridge University.' The compromise of the 'titular degree' 'left women's position in the university exactly where it was. I've never felt so bitter in my life.'[43] 'My idea of life is to have enormous quantities of friends, but to live alone. And I do not know whether Girton or the study of medieval nunneries did more to convince me that I was not born to live in a community.'[44]

After Eileen Power came to the LSE the predominantly literary, cultural and social framework of her history was to change under the influence of the social sciences then being fostered there. When she first came to the LSE she described herself as half-way through a major study of medieval women, from which the book on nunneries was a diversion; but now the larger book was never written. Instead, this work emerged in a number of major lectures on working women, bourgeois women, medicine and midwifery, and in the studies of the menagier's wife and the medieval nun which appeared in *Medieval People*. Her translation and edition of *The Goodman of Paris*, and her work on the family of clothiers, the Paycockes, included extended discussions of courtship, marriage and middle-class women's domestic lives.[45]

One major influence on Eileen Power's work from the time she went to the LSE was her great political commitment to the peace movement, and subsequently, from the mid-1930s, to the anti-appeasement movement. For during and after the war, Eileen Power, like many women who had campaigned for the vote, now joined peace organisations such as the League of Nations Union or the Women's International League for Peace and Freedom. She fostered the study of social and economic history and international and comparative history in the universities and the schools. Eileen Power saw this as her great contribution to the cause of the League of Nations. European and world history, and especially social history, would help to create a community with common historical ideas and with a sense of the likeness between nations. This was the framework for her most famous work, *Medieval People*, for her article 'A Plea for the Middle Ages' and for her research projects afterwards.[46]

When Eileen Power came to the LSE she worked closely with R. H. Tawney. Together they had worked out the courses of study which created the discipline of economic and social history during the 1920s and 1930s. Tawney had a profound influence on her; he was the socialist prophet who gave vision and purpose to her history. Tawney chose a personal engagement with the processes of history to explore fundamental truths. Eileen Power never had his religious sensibility, but she developed a framework of lectures on the medieval economy which focused, like Tawney's own lectures, on the early modern economy, on international connections, trade, merchants and manufacturers and travellers. And Tawney found in Eileen Power the energy, humanism and personal inspiration that made social and economic history as it flourished in Great Britain for half a century their special creation. Together they shifted the focus of economic history away from its former preoccupation with tariffs and the regulation of trade towards social, agrarian and industrial history. Together they compiled *Tudor Economic*

Documents, and they pursued common aspirations for changes in economic history towards more sociological, comparative, analytical and international history. Together they founded the Economic History Society in 1926, and Power acted as its Secretary and key organiser until her death in 1940.[47]

The field Eileen Power entered in economic history was a new one, but it was one in which women already played a more than proportionate role in comparison with others. Lilian Knowles herself had supervised a number of women at the LSE whose names became associated with major works: Alice Clark, Joyce Dunlop, Ivy Pinchbeck, Mabel Buer, Dorothy George, Julia de Lacy Mann and Vera Anstey. Women comprised 20 per cent of the 500 people who joined the Economic History Society in 1927.[48]

Eileen Power developed the international aspects of medieval history – medieval trade, comparative economic history and world history – but she kept this history immediate and human by combining it with literary references and personal portraits. Her chapter in 1932 for the *Cambridge Medieval History*, 'Peasant Life and Rural Conditions (*c.* 1100 to 1500)',[49] succeeded in combining a large-scale comparative history of the peasantry across Europe with descriptions of village life, women's work and witches. Her work, within the framework of the social sciences at the LSE and of the international peace movement, thus turned from social and cultural history to comparative economic history and to international trade and industry.

During the 1920s and 1930s Eileen Power's research and her supervision of students focused increasingly on medieval trade and industry. During this time she also worked closely with M. M. Postan, her student, then research assistant, and later a lecturer at the LSE. Postan, a Russian émigré, arrived in England with a background of study in economics, sociology and methodology at the Universities of St Petersburg, Odessa and Kiev, and came to study economic history at the LSE. Eileen Power taught him, and after his disappointment in achieving only a second-class degree in 1924, she hired him as her research assistant, supervised his MA, then found posts for him at University College London and subsequently at the LSE. By the early 1930s they were working closely together developing new courses at the LSE, running the medieval economic history seminar, and pursuing research on the wool trade. They were both also actively seeking, through papers and working groups, to stimulate close connections between economic and social history and the social sciences. Postan was a historian with a great comparative knowledge and a middle European training in sociology and economics.

Eileen Power's own research and the Medieval Economic History Seminar she ran with Postan now traversed the terrain of merchants and clothiers, trade routes, wool farming, taxation, the staple system and politics. The great *Cambridge Economic History of Europe* which she initiated, and the first volume of which she edited with J. H. Clapham and which was published in 1941 just after her death, was perhaps the greatest testimony to the analytical, comparative and international history she fostered at the LSE. It was a far cry from the early social history which she had learned and written at Cambridge. Her own research was to result in a full-scale study of the medieval wool trade. The outlines of this were delivered in her Oxford Ford Lectures in 1939; but her sudden death in 1940 prevented completion of her book.[50]

The Medieval Economic History Seminar which she conducted with Munia Postan trained a generation of medieval economic historians; among these were a number of women including Marjorie Chibnall, Eleanora Carus-Wilson, Sylvia Thrupp, Alwyn Ruddock and Dorothy Oshinsky. It was one of the first such seminars which co-ordinated research on a single topic – medieval trade – making use of the customs accounts as a source. One of the results was her and Postan's *Studies in English Trade in the Fifteenth Century* (1933).[51]

Eileen Power's years at the LSE were marked by close friendships, and sociability. She liked the progressive views prevailing there, and the informal and friendly atmosphere. In comparison she described Oxford's academics as 'flies in amber (or are they more like prawns in aspic?)'.[52] She exchanged clerihews in the *Clare Market Review* with A. L. Bowley, the statistician: 'Holy Holy Holy, Arthur Lionel Bowley, Decomposing slowly.' His reply was: 'Eileen Power, Fair as a flower, Things will come to a pretty pass, When she withers like grass.' Her friends and close colleagues, Harold Laski, Charles Webster, Tawney and Postan, Sir Mathew Nathan, Humbert Wolfe, the Clapham family and others, gravitated to her house in Mecklenburgh Square where there were frequent dances in the large kitchen in the basement. She held many dinner parties managed by her capable housekeeper, Mrs Saville. These brought together some students, young lecturers and political figures such as Hugh Gaitskell and Evan Durbin with writers, including H. G. Wells, publishers, and visitors from the USA, China and many other countries. She frequented the Gargoyle Club, the Soho nightclub favoured by London's bohemian intellectuals, until she resigned after the Club refused to allow her to take in Paul Robeson when he was visiting London. She was a part of literary London, publishing often in the weeklies, and was loosely connected to Bloomsbury. Neither did she give up her friends in Cambridge. She spent most summer vacations working in Cambridge, staying either in Girton or with the Claphams, and she took many holidays with her old friend M. G. Jones.

She stood out among contemporary academic women as a tall, slim figure, between 5 foot 6 and 5 foot 7 with classic good looks. She was described by John K. Fairbank, the Harvard Professor and historian of China, as 'a remarkable phenomenon . . . she had a Meryl Streep kind of startling good looks, except perhaps a firmer jaw. But her primary characteristic was that she had an LSE mind (I mean this as high praise in the 1920s). She was incisive and intellectually well organized and rather made a point of being well dressed.'[53] Eileen Power fostered a reputation for a taste in exotic and designer clothes. On the publication of an article, she was said to reward herself with a flight on Imperial Airways from Croydon Airport to Paris to buy a new outfit.[54] J. H. Clapham recalled commenting to her at some learned gathering: 'Eileen, you look like Semiramis.' She had replied, 'I thought I looked like a Professor of Economic History.'[55]

In 1937 Eileen Power married Michael ('Munia') Postan, who was by then a lecturer in economic history in Cambridge and a Fellow of Peterhouse. She was then aged 47, and he approximately ten years younger. The marriage was a shock to many because of the difference in their ages, their positions and their physical appearance. Eileen's housekeeper, Mrs Saville, on hearing of the marriage, said, 'I don't like to think of Miss Eileen being walked over at her age, but these foreigners are rather good at it.'[56] A few months later Clapham's Chair in Economic History at the LSE was advertised. Eileen Power was urged to apply and Clapham expected she would be appointed.[57] But this was the chair she had long considered a suitable one for Postan, and she stepped aside in favour of him.

Eileen Power had fostered his career, and long prepared him for this post. She wrote to him in 1932:

> Clapham's chair will be vacant in about 7 years' time. You can't get a chair in London or Oxford, because you are blocked by myself and Clark; but I have for some time had my eye on Cambridge for you. It is a snag that you are not a Cambridge man; but as far as I can see there aren't going to be any Cambridge men available, for Clapham has failed to train up any successor of the right calibre . . . It depends entirely on how big a reputation you can amass in the next 7 years, & on how we manage Clapham.[58]

When the time came Eileen Power stepped aside, with the excuse that she preferred living in London.

> I do find the LSE a much more stimulating place to work in and London a more congenial place to live in than Cambridge . . . I'm not sure how I should settle down in the much more formal society of Cambridge . . . It would be an honour

to hold Clapham's chair (tho' not more of an honour than to hold Mrs Knowles's) – and I know that it would be a good thing from the point of view of the position of women for one of us to get it.[59]

After their marriage they commuted between the house in Mecklenburgh Square Eileen Power had lived in since 1922, and a new architect-designed house they had built at 2 Sylvester Road in Cambridge. But the commuting was soon to go into reverse after the beginning of the war, for Postan was appointed to the Ministry of Economic Warfare and went to London, and the LSE was evacuated to Cambridge. Eileen took two LSE students into her house as evacuees. The dinner parties and dances once held in Mecklenburgh Square were now replaced in Cambridge by Sunday afternoon 'at homes' for economic historians and a mixture of others from Cambridge and London.

Eileen Power gathered many honours over the course of her career. She was given an Honorary D.Litt. in 1933 by Manchester University and by Mount Holyoke College in 1937. She gave the Founder's Memorial Lecture in Girton in 1936 with a paper on 'Pastoral England in the Middle Ages'. She became a corresponding member of the Medieval Academy of America in 1936, and was the first woman to give the Ford Lectures in Oxford in 1939. These lectures were published after her death as *The Wool Trade in English Medieval History*.

Eileen Power died suddenly in London of a heart attack in August 1940. Her death was a great blow to her friends, colleagues and students, for as a personality, a teacher and an initiator of research, she had been so much more than the books and articles she wrote. She left much unfinished, but by the time of her death she held a central place in the creation of the new discipline of economic and social history, and in making this history a major part of the national culture during the inter-war years.

NOTES

1 J. H. Clapham, 'Eileen Power, 1889–1940', *Economica* 20 (1940), 355–9; M. G. Jones, 'Memories of Eileen Power', *Girton Review* 114 (1940), 3–13.

2 *The Times*, Criminal Courts, 29 April 1905.

3 Ellen McArthur (1862–1927) was educated at St Leonard's School under Louisa Lumsden, and lectured in economic history in Cambridge between 1902 and 1912. She was Director of Studies in History when Eileen Power came up to Girton, but left in that year to supervise the History Department at Westfield College. See M. B. Curran, 'Ellen Annette McArthur, 1862–1927', *Girton Review* 75 (1927), 83–103.

Winifred Mercier (1875–1925) was trained for school-teaching and taught for five years in Scotland. From here she went to Somerville in 1904, and completed a degree in Modern History. She returned to teaching at Manchester High School, and in 1909 went to Girton as Director of Studies in History. She stayed at Girton until 1913, then went into teacher training at Leeds City Training College. She became Principle of Whitelands Training College in 1916, and pursued educational reform until she died in 1925. See Lynda Grier, *The Life of Winifred Mercier* (Oxford 1937), and 'Winifred Mercier', *Time and Tide* (17 July 1925), 695–6.

4   Power Papers, Cambridge University Library.

5   See letters from Eileen Power to Margery Garrett, and the diary Eileen Power kept during her year in Paris in 1910–11. Both are in the Power Papers held by Lady Cynthia Postan. These are hereafter referred to as Postan Papers to distinguish them from papers in the Cambridge University Library and in Girton College.

6   Alon Kadish, *Historians, Economists and Economic History* (London 1989), p. 149; Rita McWilliams-Tullberg, *Women at Cambridge* (London 1975), p. 88; E. E. C. Jones, *As I Remember: an Autobiographical Ramble* (London 1922), p. 55.

7   Dora Russell, *The Tamarisk Tree: My Quest for Liberty and Love* (London 1975), p. 35.

8   Russell, *The Tamarisk Tree*, p. 35.

9   Eileen Power to Margery Garrett, n.d., 1910, Postan Papers.

10 Eileen Power to Margery Garrett, n.d., 1910, Postan Papers; Newnham College, Education Committee Minutes, 28 April 1910, Newnham College Archives.

11 Power to Margery Garrett, 6 November 1910, Power Papers held by Lady Cynthia Postan.

12 Power to Garrett, 26 March 1911.

13 Eileen Power to Margery Garrett, 17 May 1911, Power Papers.

14 Power to Margery Garrett, 22 July 1911, Postan Papers in possession of Lady Cynthia Postan.

15 Ibid. Eileen Power was interviewed for the Fellowship by Hubert Hall. Charlotte Shaw, a Fabian and wife of G. B. Shaw, provided the funding for the Fellowship, and set the topics. See Shaw, Research Studentship file, BLPES. I owe this point to Carol Dyhouse.

16 Eileen Power, *Medieval English Nunneries, c. 1275–1535* (Cambridge 1922).

17 Power to MLG, 9 July 1912; Power to MLG, August 1912.

18 Power to MLG, 13 September 1912, 17 November 1913, 21 July 1914, 16 March 1915.

19 Power Papers, Girton College Archives.

20 Eileen Power to G. G. Coulton, 5 September 1920, Power Papers, Girton College Archives.

21 'A Melancholy Chronicle', *New Statesman* 20 (27 January 1923), 412; 'Medieval People', *Times Literary Supplement* (11 September 1924), 551; Bertha H. Putnam, 'Medieval English Nunneries', *American Historical Review* 29 (1924), 538–9.

22 Power, 'The Menagier's Wife, a Paris Housewife in the Fourteenth Century', in Power, *Medieval People* (1924), London 1986, pp. 96–120; Power, 'The Working Woman', in Power, *Medieval Women*, ed. M. M. Postan (Cambridge 1975), pp. 62–70.

Power has since been criticised for her failure adequately to set out the extent of these women's subordination in spite of their contributions. See J. M. Bennett, '"History that Stands Still": Women's Work in the European Past', *Feminist Studies* 14 (1988), p. 270; Olwen Hufton, 'Women in History: Early Modern Europe', *Past and Present* 101 (1983), pp. 38–41.

23 Power to MLG, 25 September 1914.

24 Power to MLG, 21 January 1915.

25 Power to MLG, 16 March 1915.

26 Power to MLG, 25 September 1918.

27 Power to MLG, 16 March 1915.

28 Power to MLG, 7 July 1917.

29 Dora Russell, *The Tamarisk Tree*, p. 36.

30 Power to MLG, 10 June 1917.

31 Dorothy Marshall, Diaries. Dorothy Marshall (1900–94) was taught by Power at Girton as an undergraduate from 1918 to 1920, and was supervised by her later at the LSE. She did research on the Poor Law, then lectured at Bedford College for four years, followed by a two-year appointment at Durham. She went to a History appointment at the University of Cardiff in 1936, and stayed there until her retirement in 1967. She was the author of several books, among them, *The English Poor in the Eighteenth Century: a Study in Social and Administrative History* (London 1926); *The Rise of George Canning* (London 1938); and *English People in the Eighteenth Century* (London 1956).

32 'Memories of Eileen Power at Girton' by Mary Llewelyn Davies and Theodora Calvert, Girton College Archives.

33 Ibid.

34 Power to MLG, 22 September 1916.

35 Dora Russell, *The Tamarisk Tree*, pp. 35–6.

36 Eileen Power, 'Women of Cambridge', *The Old Cambridge* (14 February 1920), p. 11.

37 Power to MLG, 26 February 1917, 25 September 1918.

38 Power to MLG, 24 September 1914, August 1912.

39 Power to Coulton, 27 April 1920.

40 Eileen Power, Travel Diary, 'Tour du monde', 1, 21 December 1920, Postan Papers.

41 Eileen Power, *Alfred Kahn Travelling Fellowships. Report to the Trustees September 1920–September 1921* (London 1921), pp. 49–55. Cf. G. L. Dickinson, *Letters from John Chinaman* (London 1901).

42 Power to Coulton, 5 September 1925, Power Papers, Girton College.

43 Power to MLG, 21 July 1921, Postan Papers; Eileen Power to Bertrand Russell, 20 October 1921, Russell Papers, McMaster University.

44 Power to Coulton, 30 January 1922, Power Papers, Girton College.

45 Power, *Medieval People*, pp. 73–95, 152–73; Power, *The Paycockes of Coggeshall* (London 1920); Power, *The Goodman of Paris: a Treatise on Moral and Domestic Economy by a Citizen of Paris c. 1393* (London 1928).

46 Power, *A Bibliography for Teachers of History* (London 1919), published by the
    Women's International League; Power, 'A Plea for the Middle Ages', *Economica* 5
    (1922), 173–80; Power, 'An Introduction to World History', unpublished typescript of
    book, Postan Papers held by Lady Cynthia Postan.

47 R. H. Tawney and Eileen Power, *Tudor Economic Documents* (London 1924); D.
    Ormrod, 'R. H. Tawney and the Origins of Capitalism', *History Workshop* 18 (1984),
    138–59; J. M. Winter, 'Introduction', in Winter (ed.), *History and Society: Essays by
    R. H. Tawney* (1978), pp. 1–35; Tawney, 'Eileen Power', address delivered at Golders
    Green Crematorium, 12 August 1940 (1940).

48 See Maxine Berg, 'The First Women Economic Historians', *Economic History Review*
    45 (1992), 314–15.

49 Power, 'Peasant Life and Rural Conditions *c.* 1100–1500', in *Cambridge Medieval
    History* VII (Cambridge 1932), pp. 716–50.

50 Power with J. H. Clapham, *Cambridge Economic History of Europe*, I (published post-
    humously, Cambridge 1941); correspondence between J. H. Clapham and Eileen
    Power about the *Cambridge Economic History*, Postan Papers; Power, *The Wool Trade
    in English Medieval History* (Ford Lectures, published in Oxford posthumously, 1941).

51 The studies eventually emerging from the group of students who attended the
    Power–Postan seminar include Sylvia Thrupp, *The Merchant Class of Medieval London*
    (Ann Arbor 1948); Alwyn Ruddock, *Italian Merchants in Southampton* (London 1951);
    E. M. Carus-Wilson and O. Coleman, *England's Export Trade, 1275–1547* (Oxford
    1963); E. M. Carus-Wilson, *Medieval Merchant Venturers* (London 1967); M. K. James,
    Studies in the Medieval Wine Trade (Oxford 1971).

52 Power to Postan, 26 February 1932, Postan Papers.

53 Cited in W. H. McNeill, *Arnold Toynbee a Life* (Oxford 1989), p. 310.

54 Interview with Sir Michael Clapham and Miss Barbara Clapham, 21 July 1993.

55 J. H. Clapham, 'Eileen Power, 1889–1940', *Economica* 20 (1940), 355–9.

56 Interview with Sir Michael Clapham and Miss Barbara Clapham, 21 July 1993.

57 Power to Helen Cam, 6 January 1938, Power Papers, Girton College Archives; inter-
    view with Miss Barbara Clapham, 21 July 1993.

58 Power to M. M. Postan, 29 January [1932], Postan Papers.

59 Power to Helen Cam, 6 January 1938, Power Papers, Girton College Archives.

*

All the essays published in *Medieval Women* are based on manuscript lectures and
papers in Eileen Power's hand, and at least partly annotated by her. These are
available in the Postan/Power papers in Cambridge University Library.

This foreword originally appeared as Chapter 7, 'Eileen Power, 1889–1940' by
Maxine Berg, in *Cambridge Women: Twelve Portraits*, edited by Edward Shils and
Carmen Blacker (Cambridge: Cambridge University Press, 1996), pp. 159–82.

Preface

From the very outset of her career as a scholar Eileen Power was engaged on a history of women in the Middle Ages. Her ambition was to produce a study fuller and better grounded in evidence than any of the existing books on the subject. At times other subjects, above all the medieval wool trade, claimed much of her time and interest, but she never ceased to collect material or to produce summaries of evidence for her study of medieval women. Her *Medieval Nunneries*, and her editions of *The Goodman of Paris* and *The Miracles of the Blessed Virgin Mary* were by-products of this pre-occupation; but a by-product greater in bulk and perhaps wider in appeal was the popular lectures on the subject she gave at different times in Cambridge, at the London School of Economics, in the USA, and on the radio. With the possible exception of a chapter in *The Legacy of the Middle Ages* (OUP 1926) these popular essays remained unpublished, but having heard or read them, and having occasionally shared in their composition, I always toyed with the idea of assembling them for publication. What held me back was the hope that one day I should find time, or could induce someone else, to take over Eileen's collection of notes and drafts and complete her main project. I feared that until and unless the latter's future was secured, the publication of Eileen Power's popular versions might prejudice its chances. Fortunately last year Professor Eleanor Searle of the University of California, a medievalist of great distinction, agreed to take on the job, and by doing so, removed my main objection to the immediate publication of the lectures.

Hence the present book. With the exception of Chapter 3, which Eileen largely based on my researches and in which she embodied numerous passages written by me, the book is largely made up of texts Eileen Power composed herself. Yet the book itself was not assembled by Eileen Power. Her texts were available in several variants; to make a book I had to select the versions which appeared to combine best and, so to speak, to sew them together. But in doing this I was able to preserve Eileen Power's original versions with very few changes of substance or wording. Only in those passages in which her facts appeared to be at variance with results of more recent researches, did I allow myself to correct them in the text or in end notes.

The notes are, of course, all mine; so is the bibliography. The latter, as befits a popular book, is highly selective. It does not list any contemporary record evidence (such a list would have comprised most of the existing collections of records) and is confined to books non-specialist readers may wish and be able to consult. More comprehensive – at least in intention – are the endnotes. In compiling them I tried to identify the sources of all Eileen Power's citations and references to authorities, and was able to do so in all but very few instances.

The illustrations have been selected by Miss Anne Boyd of CUP who has also seen the book through the press.

I received help and advice from a number of friends and colleagues, above all from Professor David Knowles, an old and intimate friend of both Eileen and myself. He read and commented on the first draft and encouraged me to publish the book. He died just as I was on the point of writing to him to ask for permission to cite his name in this preface.

M. M. POSTAN

Medieval ideas about women

I

The position of women is often considered as a test by which the civilisation of a country or age may be judged. The test is extraordinarily difficult to apply, more particularly to the Middle Ages, because of the difficulty of determining what in any age constitutes the position of women. The position of women is one thing in theory, another in legal position, yet another in everyday life. In the Middle Ages, as now, the various manifestations of women's position reacted on one another but did not exactly coincide; the true position of women was a blend of all the three.

It is nevertheless worth while to consider the first of these manifestations in isolation, for the medieval theory about women, bequeathed as a legacy to future generations and enshrined alike in law and in literature, was destined to have profound social effects for centuries to follow, long after the forces behind it had ceased to be important and when the conditions which had accounted for it no longer existed.

In considering the characteristic medieval ideas about woman it is important to know not only what the ideas themselves were but also what were the sources from which they sprang. The expressed opinion of any age depends on the persons and the classes who happen to articulate it; and for this reason alone it often represents the views of a small but vocal minority. In the early Middle Ages what passed for contemporary opinion came from two sources – the Church and the aristocracy. In other words, the ideas about women were formed on the one hand by the clerkly order, usually celibate, and on the other hand by a narrow caste, who could afford to regard its women as an ornamental asset, while strictly subordinating them to the interests of its primary asset, the land. Indeed, it might with truth be said that the accepted theory about the nature and sphere of women was the work of the classes least familiar with the great mass of womankind.

It was these classes who determined the concept of marriage which prevailed far into the nineteenth century and who established the status of women under the law. Since they were in agreement in placing woman in subjection to man, neither the concept of marriage nor the law took note of her as a complete individual, as what Maitland calls 'a free and lawful person'. The fact which governed her position was not her personality but her sex, and by her sex she was inferior to man. On the other hand, it was these very classes who developed, with no apparent sense of incongruity, the counter-doctrine of superiority and the adoration which gathered round the persons of the Virgin in heaven and the lady on earth and which handed on to the modern world the powerful ideal of chivalry.

Both these divergent dogmas owed something to forces outside the age which enunciated them. They derived in part from the Pauline system of Christian values, from the Roman idea of tutelage and from the Teutonic concept of authority in family (the *mund*), and also borrowed something from the Arab idea of chivalry.

In short, the characteristic medieval attitude could only have arisen in an age in which clerical and aristocratic groups were able to impose their point of view on society. If public opinion had been formed from the bottom upward, rather than from the top downward, the prevalent dogma might have been different. It might have been different even had it taken account of the attitude of the wealthier members of the urban middle classes. However, the voices of the Church and the aristocracy, resonant and all-pervading though they were, did not wholly submerge some other voices. Above all, the upper ranks of urban middle classes were making themselves increasingly heard, from the twelfth century onwards, as trade developed and towns grew. Their views of women betrayed a better understanding of women's real position in medieval life than did the views of either the aristocracy or the Church. Town law had to take account of women active in trade, more particularly of married women carrying on trade on their own, as *femmes soles*. The urban regulations of *femmes soles* were often intended to protect the husbands, but in doing so they often helped to improve the status of women.

This urban note, however, though often sounded could not do much to reduce the predominance of the ecclesiastical or knightly themes. The bourgeoisie rose to importance at a time when the prevailing outlook had already been cast into certain moulds. It therefore took over the 'official' ideas about women and marriage as a dispensation of nature. Indeed the bourgeois notions in literature were often more hostile to women than the clerical ones. They were certainly more hostile than the courtly code, which as we shall see presently, made use of romance to cover up the assumed inferiority of woman. For, except in the families of great merchants able to move in aristocratic circles, urban classes did not cultivate the knightly notion of courtly service (*Frauendienst*). Indeed the period when the urban classes were at the height of their prosperity and influence, that is in the late thirteenth and the early fourteenth centuries, saw the waning of the purer ideals of knightly service and courtly love and a resurgence, in the famous rhymed stories known in France as *fabliaux*, of a secular anti-feminism as brutal as anything which the Fathers of the Church had propounded.[1]

Nevertheless the woman of *fabliaux*, odious as she is, shows something of the practical equality which prevailed between men and women in the middle classes. The woman is in subjection, but the subjection is very imperfectly maintained, and the henpecked husband is a suspiciously favourite theme. It is a poetic justice that a man, whose ideal wife was a Patient Griselda, should find himself not infrequently married to the Wife of Bath. Mysogynists there were in all ages, but diatribes against women and marriage, conspicuous in the literature of the later Middle Ages, have a different note from the bitter and yet somewhat academic attack of earlier churchmen. They are genuine pictures drawn from real life, the real twinge of the pinching shoe.

It thus appears that the medieval ideas about women as formulated by two classes in power in the early Middle Ages were only slightly modified (and that sometimes for the worse) by a class which rose to eminence during the last three centuries of the period. Yet even in this later period two great bodies of opinion were still unheard. The working classes whose labour sustained both Church and aristocracy, and who may have outnumbered the bourgeoisie in towns, remained inarticulate. The common folk, of whom we catch innumerable glimpses in the records of manors or boroughs, rarely uttered a word above the whistle of a scythe or the hum of a loom. As we shall see presently, these labouring folk were used to the sight and to the companionship of working women in fields and at benches; yet they went to their churches on Sundays and listened while preachers told them in one breath that woman was the gate of hell and that Mary was Queen of heaven On feast days, or on their visits to markets and fairs, they gathered round the *jongleurs* and laughed at the *contes gras*, or *fabliaux* in which women were ridiculed. It was only in moments of revolt, when their own voices suddenly burst out in defiance, that they refused to see Eve as a betrayer of humanity,

1 *When Adam delved, and Eve span*

forever beneath man's foot. Instead they asked

> When Adam delved, and Eve span,
> Who was then a gentleman?

Needless to say, women themselves remained all but inarticulate. We hardly ever hear of women's views of themselves. As the Wife of Bath complained, all the books were written by men.

> Who peyntede the leoun, tel me who?
> By god, if wommen hadde writen stories
> As clerkes han with-inne hir oratories,
> They wolde han writen of men more wikkednesse
> Than all the mark of Adam may redresse.

Literary works by women are rare, apart from the love letters of Heloïse or the outpourings of great women mystics and a few writings of learned nuns. Such poetesses as the troubadour Countess Beatrice of Die, and the famous writer of *lais* known as Marie de France, conform closely to the poetic convention of the day. It is not until the end of the fourteenth century that there appears a woman writer determined and able to plead for her sex and to take a stand against the prevalent denigration of women. That woman was the great Christine de Pisan of whom more will be said later.

4

2 *Christine de Pisan*

Christine was, of course, in many ways exceptional. She was a master of all the courtly conventions and was also able to make a living by her pen. Her famous attack on *Le Roman de la Rose* is infused with lofty idealism; but also reveals her exceptional knowledge of real life. The same feeling for real life shows in her description of her own happiness with her husband before he left her a young widow with a family to support; it shows too in the educational treatise *Le Livre des Trois Vertus*, which she wrote for the use of women.[2]

2

Such were the sources from which came the articulate opinion of the Middle Ages about women. They were socially restricted, and the outlook they reflected was bound to be narrow and uniform. Yet its uniformity and consistency was not as thorough as it may at first sight appear. It harboured differences of view and was subject to conflicts and fluctuations. The Church and the aristocracy were often at odds with each other; and sometimes each was at odds with itself. In both the ecclesiastic and aristocratic traffic of ideas the position of women was perpetually shunted between pit and throne. In its views of women, the Church paid little heed to the biblical injunction against halting between two opinions. Janus-faced, it looked at woman out of every sermon and treatise, yet never knew which face to turn on her. Who was the true paradigm of the feminine gender, the woman *par excellence*: Eve, wife of Adam, or Mary, Mother of Christ? On the one hand there is the image of woman as conceived by men like Jacques de Vitry (d. 1240)[3]

> 'Between Adam and God in Paradise there was but one woman and she had no rest until she had succeeded in banishing her husband from the garden of delights and in condemning Christ to the torment of the Cross.'

But on the other hand, there were views of woman represented by a manuscript in the Cambridge University Library:

> 'Woman is to be preferred to man, to wit in material: Adam made from clay and Eve from side of Adam; in place: Adam made outside paradise and Eve w'in; in conception: a woman conceived God which a man did not do; in apparition: Christ appeared to a woman after the Resurrection, to wit the Magdalene; in exaltation: a woman is exalted above the choirs of angels, to wit the Blessed Mary.' St Bernadine even declares thus: 'It is a great grace to be a woman: more women are saved than men.'[4]

Both ideas entered into the Church tradition and both wrought their influence on the medieval mind. The view of woman as instrument of the Devil, a thing at once inferior and evil, took shape in the earliest period of

3 *The evil of Eve. The temptation*

4 *The expulsion from Paradise*

Church history and was indeed originated by the Church. Its roots lay not in the words of Christ but in those of St Paul, and it found its expression in the lives and writings of the early Christian fathers and its embodiment in the ethics and philosophy of monasticism. As ascetic ideals rose and flourished, and monasticism became the refuge of many of the finest men, in the turmoil of the Dark Ages, there came inevitably into being the concept of woman as supreme temptress, *janua diaboli*, the greatest of all obstacles in the way of salvation. Indeed so great it was that even matrimony could not wholly surmount it. Some ecclesiastical writers and divines rate matrimony among the lower, the debased, conditions of human life. The sole argument which St Jerome could find in its favour was that it served to provide the world with virgins. Monasticism may have offered a refuge for some women; but the refuge merely sealed the degradation of women in general by confining full approbation to those who withdrew themselves from the world.

This attitude established a point of view about women which survived long after the social and intellectual conditions which created it had passed away. Its influence was not, of course, commensurate with its place in the official doctrines of the Church. People continued marrying and giving in marriage and invoked the blessing of the Church upon their unions. But daily practice could not escape altogether the pressures of doctrine. The clergy who preached the ascetic ideal were for many centuries the only educated and therefore the only articulate section of the community. The monastic point of view was bound to permeate the thought and the morals of society as a whole. Tertullian and St Jerome took their place with Ovid in that 'book of wikked wyves' which the Wife of Bath's fifth husband was wont to read aloud nightly with such startling results.

Turning from the Church to the aristocracy it is clear the laity as a whole took over with complacency the Church's dogma of the subjection of women. Implicit obedience was part of the ideal of marriage set out in the majority of didactic works addressed to women. Even such a loving and sensible bourgeois husband, as the Menagier de Paris, likens the wife's love of husband to fidelity of dog for master and declares that all his orders, just and unjust, important and futile, reasonable and unreasonable, must be obeyed. The same idea of wifely condition and duty is set forth in stories of 'Patient Griselda' and 'The Nut Brown Maid'; and is summarised exactly in Katharina's famous last speech in *The Taming of the Shrew*.[5] Disobedient wives were liable to correction by force. Canon law specifically allowed wife-beating, and judging by *chansons de geste* and by anecdotes related by the

5 *The temptation of St Antony*

6 *Wife-beating*

7 *Turning the tables*

Knight of La Tour Landry for the edification of daughters, such punishments were practised in the highest of circles.[6]

This ethical and social attitude to marriage was not much relieved by the specifically feudal concept of marriage. In feudal law a woman could be endowed by land, and we know of endowable women holding land by every title recognised by law, including the most exalted ones. But in practice, feudal marriage carried with it a certain denigration of woman as a person. While the Church subordinated woman to her husband, feudalism subordinated her to her fief. All feudal marriages of convenience were dictated by interests of land. In some ways an heiress – indeed an heir too – was as much a chattel tied to the soil as was the manorial villein.

In this way both Church and aristocracy combined to establish the doctrine of the woman's subjection, a doctrine which was apt to be linked with the notion of her essential inferiority. On the other hand both the Church and the aristocracy asserted, with no apparent sense of inconsistency, the counter-doctrine of the superiority of women. The cult of the Virgin and the cult of chivalry grew together, and both rose conspicuously to the surface from some time in the twelfth to the end of the thirteenth centuries when medieval culture reached its highest point. Both were perhaps signs of a reaction – this time a romantic reaction – against the sombre realities of an earlier and cruder age. Just as in the nineteenth century the Romantic movement followed on the 'age of reason' and the Revolution it inspired, so in the Middle Ages the turbulence of the Dark Ages was succeeded by the age of chivalry and of the Virgin.

The succession found its most characteristic expressions in the cult of the Blessed Virgin Mary. It spread with great rapidity and soon pervaded every manifestation of popular creed. It was already supreme by the eleventh century and remained supreme until the end of the Middle Ages. Great pilgrimages to the Virgin's shrines, Chartres, Rocamadour, Mont Saint-Michel, Laon, Soissons, Ipswich, Walsingham, and many scores more, criss-crossed the countries of Europe, while most great churches, not specifically her own, provided themselves with Lady Chapels. Her name was given to wild flowers in the fields – to Virgin's Bower and others – and English children were taught to observe how 'winking Mary-buds begin to ope their golden eyes'. Her miracles were on every lip, were enshrined in innumerable images and recorded in manuscripts and books of which the Herolt collection is the most complete and best known. They also provided the stock themes for miracle plays.[7] The Church established feasts to commemorate various incidents of her life, and Saturdays were specially assigned for her worship.

The very fall of humanity through Adam now became a matter for congratulation. Had it not been for the fall mankind could not have seen the Virgin enthroned in heaven.

> Ne hadde the appil take ben
> The appil taken ben,
> Ne hadde never our lady
> A ben hevene quene
> Blessed be the time
> That appil take was
> Therefore we moun singen
> 'Deo Gracias!'[8]

Indeed it can be said that throughout the Middle Ages men saw Christ as the divine child; so, not surprisingly, the devotion of the age was lavished upon the mother who held the divine child in her arms. But in spite of its maternal and divine implications, the devotion of the Virgin Mother was often indistinguishable in form from that which the knight lavished upon the mortal lady, except that the worship of the Virgin spread more widely and was shared by greater numbers than those with ideas of chivalry. It may therefore have done more to raise the current concept of womanhood.

In a curious and perhaps indiscriminate way the cult of the Virgin extended even to embrace the woman of the Gospels wholly outside the divine family – Mary Magdalen. But the widest extension of the cult of the Virgin, and one inspiring an attitude to women wholly different from that of the early Church, was the cult of the mundane lady.[9]

The cult of the lady was the romantic counterpart of the cult of the Virgin. It was evolved by the medieval gentry and aristocracy as part of the ideal of chivalry they formed in the twelfth and thirteenth centuries. The idea finds clear expression in the refrain of French ballads of the fourteenth century 'En ciel un dieu, en terre une déesse'. In chivalry the romantic worship of a woman is as necessary a quality of the perfect knight as the worship of God; or as Gibbon puts it, 'The knight was the champion of God and the ladies – I blush to unite such discordant terms.'

The idea of knightly love could however go further than this. Its characteristic manifestation was not a general reverence for womanhood, but a wholly original concept of love which was to inspire much of the finest literature of the Middle Ages and to contribute a major theme to the twelfth-

8 *The Virgin Mary*

9 *Garlanding an illicit lover*

century Renaissance. When the shadows of the Dark Ages finally receded and the world's great age dawned anew, there emerged a new style of life in an outburst of art, learning and literature. The outburst signalled the birth of a polite society. It was a refined and somewhat idle society, one requiring leisure to cultivate finer feelings, intellectual subtleties and polished manners.

L'amour courtois which enshrined the polite society's philosophy of life first took shape and was erected into a system in Provence. During the last half of the twelfth century troubadours of the south of France devised lyric poetry of great beauty bound up with the theory of courtly love. In the course of a brief and brilliant career the new lyric and the ideal it embodied spread throughout Western Europe. Wherever it went it inspired poetry, the troubadours and trouvères of France, the Minnesingers of Germany and those of *dolce stil nuovo* of Italy; and wherever it went it received a wel-

10 *A well-born lady's pursuits: love and sport*

come from the fashionable world.[10] Its centres were a number of brilliant little feudal courts: Champagne, Blois, Flanders, Brittany, Burgundy, and the courts of Henry II of England and of his sons, 'young King' Henry, and Richard Coeur de Lion, of Louis VII of France, Frederick Barbarossa and Pedro II of Aragon. An active part in spreading the new fashion was played by a number of great ladies, who welcomed troubadours and themselves became famous exponents of the true art of courtly love. Great ladies were the main beneficiaries as well as the main clientele of the literature and art inspired by courtly love. The *romans d'aventure* of the thirteenth century embodying it were obviously written to please an audience of women, just as the *chansons de gestes* were written to please men.

Courtly love as understood in this society had certain clearly marked insignia. In the first place it was held to be impossible between husband and wife. 'Marriage is no excuse for not loving' is the first of the rules of love. It was based on the conviction that affection binding married persons – though real and valuable – had nothing in common with the sentiment of love, which might, and indeed must, therefore, be sought outside marriage. Conditions which governed feudal marriages are sufficient to explain the dogma which sounds so perverse to modern ears. It was the essence of courtly love that it should be a thing freely sought and freely given; it could not be found in the marriage of feudalism, which was so often a parental arrangement, binding children in the interests of land. Fiefs marry but men and women love. True, the adored lady was always a wife but always someone else's wife. This was one of the rules of the game.

This peculiar conception of love had another characteristic. In it the lady stood in a position of superiority towards her lover as uncontested as the position of inferiority in which a wife stood towards husband. Love was, as it were, feudalised; the lover served his lady as humbly as the vassal served his lord. He had to keep her identity secret from the world, concealing it under some fictitious name when he praised her in song. He must not only bear himself with the utmost humility towards her, showing infinite patience in the trials to which her caprices and disdains must (by all the rules) submit him, but must strive unceasingly to make himself worthy of her by the cultivation of all the knightly virtues. For it was an axiom of the theory that every admirable quality had its root in love.

The idea that only by love can man become virtuous or noble informs all the poetry of the troubadours. But moral excellence was not the only virtue grounded in love; love was also the foundation of literary perfection. The lover must sing as he sighs, and love and poetry become almost interchangeable terms. The code in which the principles of Provençal grammar and metre were summed up in the fourteenth century was called the Laws of Love.

A close association of social virtues with love, and the high position given to woman as their inspiration, are fully reflected both in the conception and in the practice of *l'amour courtois*. Love was often platonic in the accepted sense of the term, and in fact had much in common with the true platonic conception of love, in that it made love a source of infinite spiritual possibilities. This conception of platonic love is best exhibited by Italian writers, by Petrarch and above all by Dante, who raised it to its most transcendental heights. On the other hand, if it had something in common with platonism it had even more in common with scholasticism, more particularly with juristic scholasticism. It was essentially artificial, *précieux*, of the head rather

11 *Love unto death. The scroll reads: 'Vous, ou la mort'*

12 *Formalisation of love. A ceremonial kiss*

than of the heart, with rigid rules, elaborate conventions, a whole juris-
prudence of its own. The formalisation of love owed something to Ovid
and something to universal taste for disputation. As scholastics debated in
schools so poets and ladies debated in courts. Knotty problems were produced for solution; the judgments of Marie de Champagne and other great
ladies were carried far and wide. Thus, by degrees, an arduous code of the art
of love was worked out and its rules formulated. And once codified the
rules of love were to remain in force long after the high spirit which had
animated them died away.

It is obvious that a theory which regarded the worship of the lady as
next to that of God and conceived her as the mainspring of brave deeds, a
creature half romantic half divine, must have done something to counteract
the prevalent doctrine of woman's inferiority. The process of placing women
on a pedestal had begun, and whatever we may think of the ultimate value

13 *Crowning a lover*

of such an elevation, it was at least better than plunging them, as the early Fathers were inclined to do, in the bottomless pit.

Nevertheless, it is easy to exaggerate the extent to which medieval chivalry was able to elevate the actual position of women in medieval society as a whole. The exaltation of the lady was the exclusive ideal of a small aristocratic caste; those outside the caste had no part in any refining influence of the courtly ideal. It was not professed by men of other classes, nor did it necessarily apply to women of other classes. The knight was a champion of God and the ladies, and the great majority of women who were not ladies remained unchampioned. Even in the class in which it was promulgated it was often little more than a veneer, a thin overlay covering and concealing wholly different modes of behaviour. It is probable that the idea of chivalry had far more influence upon men and women of later ages than it had upon medieval life.

Courtly love itself also played a greater part in literature than it ever did in life, for we are apt to forget how narrow was the circle for which that literature was written. In the nature of things it was at once too transcendental and too artificial for ordinary consumption. Aiming as high as it did, it transfixed only for an instant and at a single point the vast target of human affairs; the average sensual world was untouched by it. Even in fashionable circles, where alone it drew breath, *l'amour courtois* was short lived. It had a civilising effect upon manners, but the fundamental sensuality beneath the superficial polish is to be seen clearly enough in many thirteenth-century books of deportment for ladies, modelled upon Ovid's *Ars Amatoria*, so severely condemned by Christine de Pisan. In the end, little was left of courtly love; what remained was courtly flirtation, a very different matter. Moreover this polished frivolity had its reverse side, in that it stimulated to still greater violence the traditional attacks upon women.

The decline of *l'amour courtois* can best be appreciated by comparing the first and the second parts of *Le Roman de la Rose*. In this elaborate allegory of lovers' pursuit, perhaps the most famous and influential poem of the Middle Ages, the first part was written by Guillaume de Lorris before 1240, and retained much of the old spirit, but the second part, finished by Jean Chopinel de Meun by 1280, was a brilliant and brutal attack upon the whole female sex. But so encyclopedic was the range of the poem, so bold its speculations and so enchanting its poetry, that it rapidly attained a popularity which outlasted the Middle Ages.[11]

From thenceforward the chorus of anti-feminist literature sounds more strongly than ever, and the courtly note is drowned by other, mostly bourgeois, voices. The bourgeois note is first heard most clearly in those popular rhymed anecdotes which the French called *fabliaux*, and in which there is hardly one which does not turn on the deceit or viciousness of woman. The old are all evil-minded hags, the wives all betray their husbands, the girls are either minxes or fools. But too much importance should not be attached to the exceedingly hostile picture of women drawn in the *fabliaux*. In all nations and at all periods there has existed a fund of anecdotes having for its subject the perfidy of women. In this respect many of the *fabliaux* were medieval only in setting. The stories which they told were often older than the Middle Ages and some of the most popular were adopted from the East or taken from the lives of Fathers. Many, too, were *contes gras* intended

14 *The Garden of Love*

only to amuse, and their social significance should not be exaggerated. But even allowing for these factors, the rancour, the intense contempt for women expressed in them at least exemplify what amused the new bourgeois society.

Attack took also other forms which are not as amusing as the *fabliaux*, but were openly polemical. There were didactic poems detailing the vices of women, *blastanges des fames*, *epystles des fames*, *blasones des fames*, which are apt to resolve themselves into a somewhat jejune game of mud slinging. Sometimes they are allegories, such as the tale of Chicheface, the mythical monster who could feed only on women obedient to their husbands, and who accordingly had had nothing to eat for 200 years. A favourite device is to praise women for all the virtues of which they are popularly alleged to be most deficient, and then contradicting the praise in the last line of each verse:

> For tell a woman all your counsayle
> And she can kepe it wonder weyll
> She had lever go quick to hell
> Than to her neighbour she wld it tell.
> *Cuius contrarium verum est.*[12]

Another device consists in calling up a long list of all the women in the Bible or in antiquity from Eve downwards who led men astray; such was the book of 'wikked wives' which the Wife of Bath's fifth husband insisted on reading to her every evening. Marriage was never condemned but was apt to be denigrated with faint praise in the writings and pronouncements of great churchmen, from (perhaps) Gregory the Great, to Hugo of St Victor and St Thomas Aquinas himself. The position which the Church assigned to marriage in the scale of human conditions is best defined by that most moderate of medieval codifiers of doctrine, Albertus Magnus. 'Continence in marriage is a good condition, but not an excellent one, since it is more excellent in widowhood and most excellent in virginity.'[13] On its part medieval literature abounds with diatribes against marriage such as *Miroir de Mariage* of Deschamps and *Quinze Joies de Mariage* ascribed to Antoine de la Sale. In particular there were a series of savage burlesques of *l'amour courtois*, such as are to be found occasionally among the later Minnesingers in Germany, in the second part of *Le Roman de la Rose* itself, and in Antoine de la Sale's romance *Le Petit Jehan de Saintré* (1459), with its courtly and charming opening and the brutal disillusionment of its close.[14] And there was of course a long series of attacks on women's dress – a somewhat different genre.

True enough, all this misogyny produced its reaction. Some of the reaction, on the part of women themselves, could go very deep and inspire a revulsion from all current modes of life. It has indeed been argued that the prominent part which women played in heretical or near-heretical movements, such as catharism, or the Order of the Béguines, was a manifestation of women's discontent with their lot in the world. But the clearest reaction against the prevailing misogynism, like that misogynism itself, will be found in literature, in poems and prose tales in praise of women. *Biens des Fames* sprang to counter the *Blastanges de Fames* and Chaucer's *The Legend of Good Women* to match the books of 'wikked wives'. Some of the apologetic writings are so sensitive of the woman's own feelings as to suggest an authorship not only pro-feminist but also female.[15] Of the poems expressing woman's own point of view the one English readers will remember is 'The Nut Brown Maid'; but an equally good example is provided by an anonymous fifteenth-century poem less well known:

> I am as light as any roe
> To preise women wher that I go.
>
> To onpreise women it were a shame
> For a woman was thy dame:
> Our Blessed Lady bereth the name
> Of all women wher that they go.
>
> A woman is a worthy thing:
> They do the washe and do the wringe;
> 'Lullay, Lullay', she dothe thee synge
> And yet she has but care and woe.
>
> A woman is a worthy wight:
> She serveth a man both daye and nyght;
> Therto she putteth all her might,
> And yet she hathe but care and woe.[16]

In the fifteenth century the controversy about women took a new turn when an attempt was made at the French Court to revive the older and purer ideal of courtly love, under the influence of Boucicault's famous *Mirror of Chivalry*, of the poetess Christine de Pisan, the unwearied champion of her sex, and of a number of lords af the Burgundian party. An order for the defence of women was founded by them, and a famous association called the Court Amoureuse was inaugurated on St Valentine's Day 1400 in honour of women and for the pursuit of poetry. Society rang with the great attack on *Le Roman de la Rose* led by Christine de Pisan, and a little later a similar literary controversy raged round Alan Chartier's poem 'La Belle Dame Sans Merci'.

Christine de Pisan's part in the affair is intriguing since she was the only woman who took a lead in the controversy, and whose contributions to it have been preserved. Married before she was fifteen and left a widow without resources at twenty-five, she had a long struggle to support her three children by her pen. She was indeed, as a French scholar puts it, the first

15 Christine de Pisan leads the way to the 'Cité des Dames'

woman who was 'man of letters' with no other support than what she could make by writing. Something of her own hard working life, honour of purpose and strength of conviction crept into her work, more especially into the two prose treatises, *La Cité des Dames* and *Le Livre des Trois Vertus*. In the first book she compiled tales to illustrate the virtues of women; the second was an educational treatise on the duties of women in different ranks of society.

Equally eloquent are the poems in which she complains of the fashionable habit of dispraising women and attacks particularly *Le Roman de la Rose*. In *Lepistre au Dieu Damour* (which was translated into English by Hoccleve) she describes the complaint of all gentle ladies to Cupid against men, who

16 *Song and dance: ladies and gentlemen dancing the 'carole'*

win their love by protestations of misery and then brag of their conquests, or else abuse all women because they have found one of them faithless. They then say women are bad, but why blame all? Some angels were proud and fell, but not all; one apostle was a traitor, but not all. Man, born of woman, should honour his mother. It is the clerks who write wicked books against them:

> A clarkes custume is whan he enditeth
> Of wommen, be it prose, rhyme or verse
> Seyn they be wicked, all honoure be the reverse.

They say no evil is equal to a woman. But women slay no men, destroy no cities, do not oppress folk, betray realms, take lands, poison and set fire, or make false contracts. They are loving, gentle, charitable, modest, discreet. Eve sinned, but she was betrayed, and Adam was just as bad. 'Telleth on this was he not changeable?' Should not all women be honoured for the sake of the Virgin Mary? Where in the gospels is there any mention of women who forsook Jesus?

Such then were the contradictory ideas about women formulated during the Middle Ages and handed on as a legacy to future generations. On the one hand stood subjection, on the other worship; both played their part in placing women in the position they occupied in the Middle Ages, and in dictating or modifying the conditions of their existence in subsequent ages. Yet we should be wrong to consider either of these notions as the primary force in determining what the average medieval man thought about woman. A social position is never solely created by theoretical notions; it owes more to the inescapable pressure of facts, the give and take of daily life. And the social position which these facts created in medieval society was neither one of superiority nor of inferiority, but one of rough and ready equality. For in daily life man could not do without woman; he relied on her for the comfort of his home, and much more than at many other periods in history he relied on her to look after his affairs in his absence from home. Indeed something like cameraderie is to be found at times even in the writings of churchmen about women, as when Peter Lombard proclaimed that God did not make woman from Adam's head, for she was not intended to be his ruler, nor from his feet, for she was not intended to be his slave, but from his side, for she was intended to be his companion and his friend. Above all it is to be found in the part which women in fact played in daily life.[17]

CHAPTER 2

The lady

I

In the medieval world the lady of the upper classes was important in more ways than one. In the ideal of chivalry she was the adored one, the source of all romance and the object of all worship, who had but to command and she was obeyed, and for whom all deeds of valour were performed. In law and in the fabric of feudal society she was primarily important as a land-owner. In the family she was important as wife and mother, wielding great practical authority, not only in her own sphere of the home, but in a much wider sphere as her husband's representative during his absence.

Something has already been said here about the position of the woman in chivalry. What books have been written about the medieval woman (including such good books in English as Wright's *Womankind in Western Europe*) have almost all been concerned mainly with her courtly aspect, and have been based almost entirely upon romances.[1] These books bring most readily to mind the image of the lady in her complicated love affairs, half formal and half passionate; or else in her amusements, playing interminable games of chess, flying her hawk in long blue days by the river, training up young squires in the art of love and polite society, as the Dame des Belles Cousines so disastrously trained the little Jehan de Saintré; or queening it at tournaments, one of the

> store of ladies whose bright eyes
> Rain influence and judge the prize.

In the fourteenth and fifteenth centuries the graceful ideal still lingers, though shot already with other and sterner hues. We catch sight of it in Froissart's tale of the young bachelors who set out for France, each with a black patch over his eye, not to be removed until he had done some deed of honour for his lady; or in Edward III's Order of the Garter, or Boucicault's order of 'L'escu vert à la dame blanche'; or in Malory's *Morte d'Arthur*. We see it in the illuminated MSS. of the period, such as the famous calendar,

Très Riches Heures, which the brothers Van Limburg made for the Duc de Berry, where tall graceful ladies with high brows and elaborate headgear ride maying or pick their unfading garlands in an eternal summer:

> Forever warm and still to be enjoyed
> Forever panting and forever young,

with tall French castles pricking the sky beyond with fantastic turrets.

The lady of chivalry was indeed a beautiful, artificial figure, but never perhaps, save in the indolence of courts and great lords' castles, the figure of a real person. It is significant that her image has been drawn from romances, and the romantic poem of the Middle Ages, like the romantic novel today, often represented not reality but an escape from reality. Very often, it seems, the lady of the Middle Ages must have heard or read the tale of the 'Chatelaine de Vergi', or of the 'Roman de Tristan' or of the 'Morte d' Arthur' in much the same spirit in which the working girl of today, shut off from adventure, hangs rapt over romantic magazine stories. But sometimes out of real life there comes in the Middle Ages a *cri de coeur* which suddenly reveals a very different lady of chivalry. The Saxon reformer Johann Busch has preserved in his *Book of the Reformation of Monasteries* (1470–5) a poignant dialogue between himself and the dying Duchess of Brunswick.

'When her confession with absolution and penance was ended, I said to her "Think you, lady, that you will pass to the Kingdom of Heaven when you die?" She replied "This believe I firmly." Said I "That would be a marvel. You were born in a fortress and bred in castles and for many years now you have lived with your husband, the Lord Duke, ever in midst of manifold delights, with wine and ale, meat and venison; and yet you expect to fly away to heaven directly you die." She answered "Beloved father, why should I not now go to heaven? I have lived here in this castle like an anchoress in a cell. What delights or pleasures have I enjoyed here, save that I have made shift to show a happy face to my servants and gentlewomen? I have a hard husband (as you know) who has scarce any care or inclination towards women. Have I not been in this castle even as it were in a cell?"'[2]

How often in real life must the lady of chivalry have been not romantically unhappy, but simply bored!

17 (opposite) *Hawking*

2

On the other hand, in passing to the lady as landowner, we say goodbye to romance and meet a very real person indeed. The political and social organisation of the feudal world was entirely based upon the tenure of land, and the importance which their position as landowners gave to women in such a society is self-evident. We find that under English common law the unmarried woman or widow – the *femme sole* – was, as far as all private, as distinct from public, rights and duties are concerned, on a par with men. She could hold land, even by military tenure, and do homage for it; she could make a will or a contract, could sue or be sued. On the other hand when she married, her rights, for the duration of the marriage, slipped out of her hands. The lands of which she was tenant-in-fee at the time of her marriage, or which she might acquire later, forthwith became her husband's for the duration of the marriage. If a child were born to them, her lands became his for life, by a custom known as the 'courtesy of England'. He could then alienate them for the duration of the marriage or for his lifetime, as the case might be, though her consent was needed if he wished to do so for a longer period or in perpetuity. On his death, however, she became entitled to enjoy for life, under the name of dower, one-third of any land of which the husband was seized in fee during the marriage; and a husband could not alienate his own land, so as to bar her right of dower, save with her concurrence; and this right she retained even if she married again.

At all stages of her life the woman, considered as a landowner, was a person of importance. As a maid she sometimes owned wide acres and was a coveted prize for an ambitious landowner and a source of profit to the lord who had the right to give her in marriage. As a wife she brought her jointure with her, and while the marriage lasted it was to all intents and purposes her husband's. If she were widowed young and left childless she must be wooed again; if she was of more mature age she had her dower which alone, if she were a great lady, gave her more influence and made her a more considerable figure in her world than many a man of lesser rank or smaller possessions.

No doubt the important position which possession of land gave to women in feudal society had its disadvantages, particularly in the case of heiresses, since it tended continually to subordinate their persons to their possessions. Indifference sometimes shown to the personality of the husband in feudal marriages of the highest rank appears shocking to modern observers. 'Let

18 *The lady travelling*

me not to the marriage of true fief admit impediments' may be said to have been the dominating motive of the lord with son or daughter or ward to marry. Weddings were often arranged and sometimes solemnised when children were in their cradles. The rigour of feudal law, as Maitland has pointed out, afforded a special reason for such transactions: 'a father took the earliest opportunity of marrying his child in order that the right of marriage might not fall to the lord.' Innumerable examples might be quoted. In the great Berkeley family, Maurice, the third Lord Berkeley (b. 1289), was at the age of eight married by his father to Eva, daughter of Lord Zouch, who was about the same age, and was by her made father of a son before he was fourteen. Maurice, the fourth lord (b. 1338), also married at the age of eight to a daughter of Hugh Despenser of the same age; and the next lord

Thomas (b. 1366) married at the age of fourteen to Margaret de Lisle, aged about seven.[3] Sometimes an unlucky little heiress was bandied about, a helpless appendage of her land, from husband to husband before she had reached what we should call marriageable age. A child was held capable of consent at the age of seven, but marriage was voidable so long as the girl was under twelve and the boy under fourteen; at these ages they could, if they wished, formally dissent from it, and a number of cases of such repudiations can be collected from bishops' registers and other sources. Pressure against such an action must however have been very great, and unless formally repudiated, marriages remained valid. Indeed, English common law held that a wife could claim dower if nine years old at her husband's death; 'of what age soever her husband be, albeit he were but four years old.'[4]

Nor was it only young girls who were thus disposed of without their own consent. Grown women could also be summarily married off, unless (as not infrequently happened) they could purchase from their lords the right to marry whom they would and when they would. The kings as well as most feudal magnates reaped considerable income from fines paid by heiresses and widows for leave to choose their own husbands.

However, the penalties and disadvantages of the feudal landownership of women must not be exaggerated. The worst abuses of the system were confined to higher ranks of society and to earlier centuries of the Middle Ages. Advantages given to women by their position as landowners outweighed the disadvantages in an age in which marriage was a business contract in all classes of society and child marriage the rule rather than the exception.

3

The superior condition of the medieval lady was further exemplified in her importance as a wife. It is permissible to take the wife as strictly typical, for there was no place in feudal society for women who did not marry. Some unmarried women, it is true, found a place in the great households of the day, in attendance upon some lady of more exalted rank. Such a household is pictured in the will of Ralph de Nevill Earl of Westmoreland (1424):

'I give and bequeath to every esquire of mine who rides with me and is dwelling in my household at the time of my death, 10m. and to every valet 40s., and to every groom 20s. and to every page 6s 8d. . . . Item I give and bequeath to every gentlewoman of other degree, then being occupied in the nurture of my children 40s. And to every maid and woman then serving there 20s.'[5]

But these gentlewomen and others cannot often have remained unmarried and in attendance upon their lady. For girls of the upper class the sole alternative to marriage was the convent, and in monasticism many of them – as we shall see – found an honourable career.

What of the well-born girl who was not destined for a nunnery? We have seen that as a rule she married, that she married young and that she married the man selected for her by her father. The careful father would expect to arrange for his daughter's marriage and often to marry her off before she was fourteen. If he found himself dying while she was still a child, he would be at great pains to leave her a suitable dowry at *maritagium suum* in his will. A girl insufficiently dowered might have to suffer that disparagement in marriage which was so much dreaded and so carefully guarded against. Even in the lowest ranks of society a bride was expected to bring something with her besides her person when she entered her husband's house. Dowering of poor girls was one of the recognised forms of medieval charity, like the mending of bad roads.

Obviously, the system has little to commend it to the moderns. Modern civilisation has steadily extended the duration of childhood, and today there seems something almost tragic in the spectacle of children taking so soon upon their young shoulders the responsibility of marriage and motherhood. But it is unnecessary to suppose that the majority of feudal marriages turned out badly. It was an inhuman father who did not wish to do the best for his daughter, and it was only in the most exalted rank that the worldly concerns could entirely outweigh personal feelings. Moreover, the fact that most wedded couples began life together while both very young was in their favour. They came to each other with no very strongly marked ideas or preferences, and grew up together. The medieval attitude towards child marriages was that to which Christine de Pisan gave such touching expression, when she recalled her own happy life with a husband whom she married before she was fifteen and who left her at twenty-five an inconsolable widow with three children.

In order to appreciate the medieval lady's importance as a wife we must observe her in her home, as revealed to us not in romances but in records, and consider what manner of life she led, and what domestic responsibilities she bore.

Cyro nabuchodonofor balthafar et alexandro
Jht erte foznoz fampfone fangar et abyfat

19 *The lady at her table*

In observing the medieval lady at home we must bear in mind that in the Middle Ages the 'home' embraced a much wider sphere than at many later dates. Not only much more had to be done within the household, but, throughout the period, social and physical conditions of life, constant wars and slow communications, inevitably threw a great deal of responsibility on ladies as representatives of absent husbands. While the lord was away at court or at war, who looked after his manor and handed it back again, with all walls in repair, farming in order and lawsuits fought when he returned? And when the lord got himself taken prisoner, who collected the ransom, squeezing every penny from the estate, bothering archbishops for indulgences, selling the family plate? Or when the lord perchance got killed, who acted as executor of his will and brought up his children? The answer to these questions, in nine cases out of ten, is – his wife. She had to be prepared to take his place at any moment, were she Queen Regent or obscure gentlewoman of Norfolk like Margaret Paston. In theory there was the romantic, lovely and capricious lady of chivalry, flirting and embroidering and playing chess; in practice there was more often an extremely hard-worked woman and a very hard nut to crack for her enemies.

Christine de Pisan in *Le Livre des Trois Vertus* (*c.* 1406) sets down things which a lady or baroness living on estates ought to be able to do. She must be capable of replacing her husband in every way during his absence, 'Because that knights, esquires and gentlemen go upon journeys and follow the wars, it beseemeth wives to be wise and of great governance and to see clear, in all that they do, for that most often they dwell at home without their husbands who are at court or in divers lands.' A lady must be skilled in niceties of tenure and feudal law, in case the lord's rights were invaded; she must know all about management of estate, so as to supervise the bailiff and must understand her own métier as housewife and be able to plan expenditure wisely. The budget of a great lady, Christine suggests, should be divided into five parts: (1) almsgiving, (2) household expenses, (3) payment of officials and women, (4) gifts, (5) jewels, dresses, miscellaneous expenses as required. Good management of a housewife was sometimes worth more to the lord than income from tenants, for it was the wife's function to dispense wisely of the husband's resources according to his rank.

Christine de Pisan wrote about how a perfect lady ought to behave, and from many sources we know how this ideal of perfection was carried out in practice. We have already observed the number of cases in which the wife was appointed executrix of the husband's will, sometimes alone, sometimes in conjunction with other persons, and this in all classes of society. Sometimes a touch of sentiment enlivens the dry phraseology of a will as when Stephen Thomas of Lee (1417–18) in one of the earliest wills written in English in the Court of Probate, writes a counsel for his wife;

> More write I not unto you, but the Holy Trinity keep you now, dear and trusty wife. Here I make an end, wherefore I pray you, as my trust is wholly in you, over all other creatures, that this last will be fulfilled, and all other that I ordained at home, for all the love that ever was between man and woman.[6]

Letters tell the same tale of confidence which men reposed in the sense and capacity of their wives. The Paston Letters give a remarkable picture of a hard-headed business woman in fifteenth-century England. No one could really like Margaret Paston who bullied her daughter and kept the only soft

20 *The lady giving orders in her kitchen*

corner in her hard heart for her husband. But she was exceedingly competent and managed his property for him with the utmost success; collecting rents, keeping accounts and outwitting enemies. She even seems to have taken it as part of the day's work to be besieged in the manor and to have its walls pulled down about her ears by armed men.[7]

Margaret Paston's experiences show one particular in which ladies of the upper classes had to be ready in an emergency to take the husband's place, for in public and private wars in the Middle Ages, no one made any bones about attacking a castle occupied only by a lady whose lord was elsewhere; and ladies in this position often proved themselves adequate defenders. Scottish wars brought at least two such women to the fore. The Countess of Buchan defended Berwick Castle against Edward I, who afterwards hung her up in a cage on the ramparts for soldiers to mock; and the famous Black Agnes, Countess of Dunbar, defended Dunbar Castle against Edward III in 1338.

> ... trewe ladie without blek or blame
> Ay to hir prince, but only falt or cryme
> Into that hous wes captane all that tyme.
> Richt manfullie, as it wes rycht weill kind.
> Agane thame all the hous sche did defend.[8]

Annals of the Hundred Years War glitter with deeds of warlike ladies, from dauntless Joan of Flanders, of whom Froissart says she had 'the courage of a man and the heart of a lion', to the peasant girl, Joan of Arc.

The romantic stories of these women are matched by numerous sober accounts of other such women in official documents. Thus the Patent Rolls for 1461 tell us the story of Bokenham Castle claimed by the King by virtue of legal inquisition. The Knyvets, husband and wife, however claimed it and refused to give it up. The King sent nine commissioners and an escheator to take it expecting only formal legal proceedings, but when they entered the outer ward they found the drawbridge raised and John Knyvet's wife Alice appeared in a little tower over the inner fort of the bridge, keeping the castle with slings, parveises, fagots, timber and other armaments of war and assisted by William Toby of Old Bokenham, gentleman, and others to the number of fifty persons, armed with swords, glaives, bows and arrows and addressed them as follows: 'Maister Twyer ye be a Justice of the Peace. I require you to keep the peace, for I will not leave possession of this castle to die therefore and if ye being to break the peace or make any war to get the place of me, I shall defend me, for liever I had in such wise to die than to be slain when my husband cometh home, for he charged me to keep it.' The forces of the law retired in confusion.⁹

It was not only on exceptional occasions and in the absence of her husband that a lady found the weight of responsibility upon her shoulders. True, duties as a mother in some ways weighed less heavily upon ladies than could have been supposed. Large families were general, and the death-rate among children high, but new-born children in upper classes were commonly handed over to wet nurses. The training of the young squire often took him at an early age from his mother's society, and, in general, it was customary to send boys and girls away to the households of great persons to learn the manners of good breeding.

But if the nursery was not a great burden, house-keeping in a great house was. In the Middle Ages, as indeed in all ages prior to the Industrial Revolution, the management of a household was a much more complicated business than today, save for the fact that domestic servants were cheap, plentiful and unexacting. It was no small feat to provide clothes and food for the large families of great households, and to cater for the large numbers of their guests. What made the feat all the greater is that in the Middle Ages most necessities had to be prepared. Bread had to be baked in the bakehouse from corn often grown and ground on the manor, ale brewed in the brewhouse, butter and cheese made in the dairy. In the larder candles were made, bacon cured and winter meat salted down. In every manor larder there stood great salting tubs, and every manorial housewife had to lay in her supply of salt. A lady could seldom give her family fresh meat (except game and poultry) in winter. In marvelling at rich condiments, pepper, sugar, spices with which meat dishes were heavily besprinkled in medieval kitchens, we must remember months of salt meat.

Nor was it only food which had to be prepared at home. Some at least of the napery used and cloth worn by the household were spun and woven there, even at a time when the expanding cloth industry made it possible to buy stuff more cheaply in greater variety outside.

The task of lady of the manor was not only to supervise the manufacture of foodstuffs and clothing which could be made on the spot, but also to look ahead in due season and lay in household stores bought in market, shops or nearest town, or purveyed from London or some other city, or from one of the great annual fairs at Stourbridge, Boston, Winchester, St Ives, etc. Of these necessities fish, wine and spices were the most im-

21 *Ladies feasting*

portant. The Paston and Stonor Letters give many glimpses of ladies thus laying in stores, as well as of husbands in London snowed down with letters telling them to bring home '3 yards of purple shamlet for the yard 4/-, a bonnet of deep murrey for 2/4, a hose cloth of yellow kersey, 4 laces of silk, 6 dozen points' and so on.

Evidently housekeeping in these days called for considerable organising ability. But the provision of food, drink and clothing within the house by no means exhausted the lady's domestic duties. When so many commodities which she needed as housekeeper were produced on the home farm, this by itself imposed additional chores. It is plain from medieval treatises that the lady was expected to supervise the home farm and, above all, the dairy. Christine de Pisan's great lady must understand the choice of labourers, the seasons for different operations, the crops suitable for different soils, the care of animals, the best markets for farm produce.

The multifarious duties and occupations of a noble lady at home did not necessarily cease with her husband's death. We have numerous instances of widows of noblemen and gentlemen, who, whether remarried or not, continued to run their large households. It was for one of these wealthy and noble widows, Margaret, Countess of Lincoln, that Robert Grosseteste, Bishop of Lincoln drew up *c.* 1240 the Rules for the government of her

22 *The disconsolate widow. Preparation of the corpse for burial*

household which are so often quoted.[10] Such great ladies often were pious and charitable, and their benefactions were large. Notable examples are Marie de St Pol, Countess of Pembroke, who did much for the order of Minoresses in England, and the Lady Margaret, mother of Henry VII whose work for education lives today.

We must end our account of the lady at home with a picture not of one of the great ladies, but of an ordinary gentlewoman, the widowed lady of the manor. There have survived from the Middle Ages some notable wills left by widows in which the whole household unrolls itself before the reader's eyes, with its beds and hangings, plate and furniture, land and cattle, tenants and servants, all set down in place and every one remembered.

For instance Dame Joan Buckland, widow, of Edgcott in Northants, who died in 1450, left in her will a detailed picture of the manor house. It contained an inventory of plate and vestments left to the parish church and a gift to the vicar of a bed of blue buckram, with hangings, feather mattress and furniture for his hall and his kitchen, together with a silver bowl. Other legacies went to men and women several of whom received complete furniture of a room. Livestock goes mainly to servants and tenants.

'As touching my horses that be here at the day of my departing I will that Richard Clarell have the best next my mortuary, Jacob the 3rd, John Cook the 4th. As touching my carthorses I would that he that keepeth them at that day have the best and 1 cow the best ... item Alyson Swayn 2 kine and 12 ewes that I have here at my departing and that she be well seen to of clothing and bedding that is necessary unto here and well rewarded ... All the remenants of my kine and my wethers that be here in this lordship, that they be spended among my tenants in meat ... Item to my shepherd at Sewell 20 wethers and 20 s.'

She leaves to each of her tenants in Edgcott a ½ qr of wheat and same of malt, and orders the rest of the wheat and malt in her barns to be divided up among neighbouring villages. Household linen is to be as carefully divided up as livestock and, after several specific legacies, the rest of 'meyny sheets' is to be divided among servants. Division of her dresses follows and we hear of two violet gowns furred with grey, a black gown furred with marten and a black gown furred with miniver; all her other gowns and kirtles are to be divided among her women servants. The woman 'next me at my departing' has 100 shillings, a bowl and two spoons and a gown furred with minks and her scrivener in London a piece of silver gilt. There are charities numerous. She leaves 20 shillings to each of four orders of friars in Oxford, Nottingham and Coventry, for requiem mass for her husband's soul and her own, sets of silver spoons to the nuns of Pinley and Cheshunt, £20 to be divided among poor men of the Fishmongers company in London and £20 to be divided among villages round the manor. Finally she orders all the silver vessels that she was wont to be served with daily, viz. twenty-six plates and thirty-two saucers, to be smitten into coin and divided among poor husbandmen in the countryside around.[11]

This may appear to be a cold, impersonal, official document, a mere list of possessions, the last source from which one would expect to reconstruct a living personality. Yet from it Dame Joan Buckland emerges as clearly as in one of those old Dutch portraits, with every fold of her dress, every wrinkle round the eyes presented. And there were many similar women in the households of the landowning nobility and gentry.

4

The domestic responsibilities and chores of a lady of the nobility and gentry were fully matched by those of a wife of a prosperous burgess.

We are fortunate in possessing several portraits of medieval burgesses' wives which show a very sensible and broad-minded view of the place of women in society. The most charming is a book known from the author as *Le Menagier de Paris*, written by a French bourgeois of the late fourteenth century for his very young wife, a mere fifteen years old. The Menagier is an old man, and the reason for his writing is that on his death she would probably marry again. He begins the treatise as usual with a long section on religious observances and on the proper behaviour and attitude of a wife towards her husband. There follows a section dealing with practical household management which gives a full-length portrait of a medieval housewife unequalled in kind by anything else in literature. The Menagier's wife must be wise in gardening and fruit-growing as well as in more purely domestic duties. She must know how to hire occasional workmen, how to deal with tradespeople, how to choose and govern her own servants. The observations of the Menagier on this last subject are delightful, and many an inexperienced mistress today might do worse than follow his advice. After assuring his wife that he will leave to her complete control of household staff, with the right of engaging, paying and dismissing them at pleasure, he goes on with a word of warning regarding the ways of housemaids in search of a place.

'Know that of those chambermaids who are out of a place, many there be that offer themselves and clamour and seek urgently for masters and mistresses; and of these take none until you first know where their last place was and send some of your people to get their character – whether they talked or drank too much, how long they were in the place, what work they were wont to do and can do, if they have homes or friends in the town, from what sort of people and what part of the country they come, how long they were there and why they left; and by their work in the past find out what hope or expectation you may have of their work in the future. And know that often such women from distant parts of the country

42

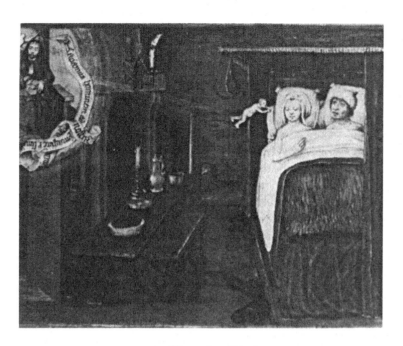

23 *The conjugal ideal*

have been blamed for some fault in their own part of the world and that is what brings them into service at a distance ... And if you find from the report of their masters and mistresses neighbours and others that a girl is what you need, find out from her and cause Master John to register in his account book the day on which you engaged her, her name and that of her father and mother and any of her kinsfolk; the place where they live and the place of her birth and her sureties ... Bear in mind the saying of the philosopher ... that if you engage a maid or man of high and proud answers you shall know that when she leaves she will miscall you if she can, and if on the contrary she be flattering and full of blandishments, trust her not – she's in league with someone else to trick you; but if she blushes and is silent and ashamed when you correct her – love her as your daughter.'

The Menagier's instructions to his wife how to look after servants after she had got them are equally practical. Good order must be maintained, quarrels and bad language prevented and morals guarded. Each servant must have his or her work assigned to her – rooms to be well swept and dusted every day, pet animals to be looked after. The Menagier's wife herself is to superintend the farm workers too and see the beasts are well cared for.

But not only is the work of servants to be superintended; she must also show great benevolence in looking after their health and happiness. She must at proper hours cause them to sit down before hearty meals with one only drink (nourishing, not intoxicating). She must admonish them to eat and drink heartily. But 'as soon as they begin to tell stories or to argue or to lean on their elbows, she must order the beguine to make them rise and take away their table – for the common folk have a saying '"When a varlet holds forth at table and a horse grazes in the ditch, it's time to take them away, for they've had enough."' In the evening they must be fed again and then (in winter) they should be able to warm themselves round the fire and be at ease. Then the wife is to lock up house and pack them off to bed: 'And arrange first that each have beside his bed a candlestick in which to put his candle and have them wisely taught to extinguish it with the mouth or the hand before getting into bed and not by throwing shirts at it.'

If she employs chambermaids of fifteen to twenty years – at this age they are foolish and don't know the world – she must cause them to sleep near her in an antechamber, or room without a skylight or low window looking onto the road, and make them get up and go to bed at your time and look after them. Also if one of the servants fall ill do you yourself, laying aside all other cares, very lovingly and charitably care for him or her and visit him and study diligently to bring about his cure'.[12]

Needless to say, in the lower orders the daily occupations of a wife greatly differed from those of wives of lords, knights or rich merchants. The woman in the labouring classes had none of the responsibilities of supervising large households or estates or employing and managing numerous servants and labourers. Her days were nevertheless occupied, equally fully if not more so, with employments and responsibilities. In her case however the employments were mostly those of bread-winning. To the woman as a bread-winner we shall now pass.

CHAPTER 3

The working woman in town and country

I

In considering the typical lady of the manor and the typical housewife of the well-to-do bourgeoisie, full account had to be taken of women's work in the home. Both among the gentry and among the bourgeoisie women did a great deal in their homes and their homes gave them great scope. The wife also had to understand her husband's job so as to take his place in his absence. The emphasis changes somewhat as we pass from the home to the labour market, from the gentry and the bourgeoisie to the working woman in town and country. As we descend the social scale, we do not find the role of women declining. On the contrary her activity, if she is alone, her importance in the life of the family, if she is married, is all the greater for the modesty, indeed exigency, of her income and possessions. In the more exalted affairs of society, the military, the diplomatic, the political, the professional, women (save on exceptional occasions) influenced events comparatively little; but they played an equal part with men in the economic life of nations. Like men, they were driven to offer themselves for hire, or otherwise to work for their living.

The appearance of women in the labour market in the Middle Ages was due to the same reason as their work today, viz. it was necessary for the married woman to earn a supplementary wage and necessary for the single woman to earn a livelihood. In every class of western society marriage is a career, to which most girls aspire. But in the Middle Ages, and often today, marriage by no means always meant that a woman devoted herself to the home and was exempt from some industry. As we shall see presently the wife of a craftsman almost always worked as her husband's assistant in his trade, or if not, she often eked out the family income by some such bye industry as brewing and spinning; sometimes she even practised a separate trade as a *femme sole*.

Moreover, not all women could hope to marry. For a variety of reasons the total number of women, then as now, was in excess of the number of

24 *The draper's shop*

men. This was due to the greater difficulty of rearing boys and possibly to the greater mortality among men in the perennial plagues of the Middle Ages; partly also to the greater risk of sudden death which they ran in wars, or town feuds, or general disturbances of the countryside; and partly to the celibacy of the large body of monks and still larger body of secular clergy whose numbers were very much greater than those of nuns. We have no reliable statistics of the total population of England; but in Germany towns took censuses which are fairly reliable. From these we know that for every 1000 adult males there were 1100 women in Frankfurt (1383), 1207 women in Nuremberg (1449) and 1246 women in Basel (1454).[1] Some outlet for the surplus female population had to be found. In the upper classes and superior ranks of the bourgeoisie this outlet was found in nunneries; in the lower classes it was found in work.

There is no doubt that in England the proportion of the two sexes was similar, and that in England as abroad unmarried women had to support themselves by work. In this respect however the lot of the unmarried woman was not exceptional, since most wives of the labouring classes 'laboured' in the same urban and rural occupations as their unmarried sisters or their husbands.

2

It may be that large numbers of women were to be found in the same occupation which before the first war provided the main employment for women, especially the unmarried ones, that is domestic service. Yet it is by no means true (as sometimes stated) that women in the Middle Ages were, as a rule, unpaid domestic workers and not wage earners. The cases in which a man was helped by his wife and daughter and perhaps maidservant in his trade were perhaps more numerous than the cases of women who carried on an independent occupation. Even gild regulations, which expressly exclude women from participation in a trade, regarded this unprofessional labour as a matter of course and made exceptions for wives and daughters. In 1372 when articles were drawn up for the leathersellers and pouch-makers of London and for dyers serving these trades, wives of dyers of leather were sworn together with their husbands to do their calling. At a time when factories were unknown and industries were carried on by craftsmen in their own homes and workshops, it was natural they should invoke the assistance of wives as well as that of apprentices and journeymen.

The fact that wives were accustomed to assist husbands in crafts is perhaps the reason why all through the later Middle Ages we find large numbers of widows carrying on their dead husbands' trade. Sometimes gild regulations specifically allow them to do so. Husbands often expected wives to carry on business after their death, for we frequently find men providing in their wills that their apprentices should serve out their term with their widows, or for leaving to their wives implements belonging to trade.

Trades thus carried on by widows ranged from that of merchants on a large scale, trafficking in ships and dealing with the Crown, to that of small craftsmen. No small amount of knowledge and ability was required to manage a large and important business; and widows doing so must have been competent folk, well able to hold their own even in the complications of foreign commerce. Instances of such women abound in our sources. In 1370 Alice late wife of John de Horsford, came into the Gildhall of London and claimed ownership of a moiety of a ship called the Seynte Mariebot of London, which had been seized by the bailiff of Billingsgate as the property of someone else. She proved title, and the court ordered delivery to be made. Another merchant's widow, Margery Russell of Coventry, was robbed of merchandise worth £800 by some men of Santander in Spain and obtained letters of marque empowering her to seize goods belonging to other Spaniards in order to recoup herself; whereupon she apparently took more than her due and the Spaniards complained against her.[2] More interesting still are the operations of one Rose of Burford, an offspring of a wealthy London family of Romaine. We encounter her during the lifetime of her husband in one of the exchequer Issue Rolls where Rose, wife of John of Burford citizen and merchant of London, received 100 marks for a cope ornamented with coral, purchased from her by Queen Isabella to make a present to the Pope. References to her husband are common. He was Sheriff of London and a rich merchant, and it is by reason of a large loan which he made the King in aid of his Scots Wars in 1318 that we first come in contact with Rose in a business capacity. For shortly afterwards her husband died, and the loan, which was to have been repaid out of issues of custom on wool and hides for the current year, was still owing. Rose as executor of the will had the job of recovering it, and we have no less than five petitions on this subject from her which have survived. Finally she ventured to suggest a remedy herself. Would the King command the debt to be allowed to her out of the customs duty which she would have to pay for her own wool which she was about to ship out of the port of London? This time she was required to come into Court and display the King's recognisances for the sum owing to her, after which the amount was allocated to her out of duty payable on her own wool. That she was carrying on business as a merchant also appears from a letter directed in 1323 by the Mayor and Corporation of the City of London to the Mayor and Corporation of Dover on her behalf, her goods having been arrested in that port for payment of a debt.[3]

Rose de Burford was not the only woman to carry on her husband's business as a wool merchant. The Hundred Rolls of 1274 mention among great wool merchants 'widows of London who make great trade in wool and other things, as Isabella Buckerel and others', and at least one woman is described as a Merchant of the Staple (and consequently an established exporter of English wool to Calais) among persons shipping wool from London in the reign of Edward IV.[4]

Widows sometimes had to account for large sums of public money if their husbands happened to be acting in an official capacity at the time of their death. The widow of Robert Baynard returns an account of temporalities of the see of Durham of which her husband was keeper during vacancy; and we know of widows responsible to the exchequer for custom accounts at various ports as executors of husbands who had acted as receivers of customs.[5]

3

It must not be supposed, however, that women's work in the labour market in the Middle Ages was confined to assisting their husbands while they were alive or carrying on their husbands' business after their death. Many unmarried women supported themselves as shopkeepers and wage earners and many married women carried on occupations of their own perfectly distinct from those of their husbands.

Girls were often apprenticed to trades in the same way as boys. The Statute of 1407 which tried (in the interest of agriculture) to confine industry to men and women possessing annual rents to twenty shillings per annum, forbade those who had not this amount to apprentice a child to a trade; and the statute specifically speaks of 'son or daughter'.[6] Wills of London citizens often leave provision for daughters as well as sons to be apprenticed. Where a gentleman of the upper class will leave a sum of money to his daughter as a dowry to wed her or to put her into a nunnery, a father in an urban occupation will leave money to wed her or put her to a trade.

Sometimes girls, as well as boys, were sent out at a very early age to work, for exploitation of child labour was by no means an invention of the Industrial Revolution. Very small children helped mothers to sort and card wool for spinning in their own homes. We recall how in 1724 Defoe praised

25 *A visit to the bank*

Yorkshire cloth-making districts because there was scarce any child there who did not work. This was not however a wholly new practice in Defoe's time and was not confined to Yorkshire. Gilds set their faces against apprentices of too tender an age, but that there were abuses appears from a case of breach of contract brought in the fourteenth century by a London cutler, one William Brewer of Holborn, and Elena his wife, asserting that a girl had been bound to serve them for seven years and had left them to go to her parents, in the course of which it was discovered by the Court that the child was three years old at the time of the alleged contract. The Statute of Labourers of 1388 (again in the interests of agriculture) forbade boys and girls who had worked at husbandry up to the age of twelve to be taken away and apprenticed to trade after that. But if apprenticed before twelve the child could remain.[7]

We find girls apprenticed to men as well as women, but more usually the assumption seems to be that female apprentices will be under tuition of the master's wife. This is only natural, when we remember that an apprentice lived in the master's house as one of the family, and was supposed to make himself generally useful, and to receive training in manners and morals and due chastisement for misbehaviour, as well as to be taught a trade. Moreover, since the wife habitually worked in her husband's shop, she could give technical as well as general instruction. In 1364 sureties were taken for Agnes, the wife of a London cutler, that she would teach Jusema her apprentice and feed and clothe her and not beat her with a stick or knife.[8] In 1376 we find an amusing record to the effect that whereas Agnes Cook was bound apprentice to William Kaly and Johanna his wife for eight years, the said William and Johanna came into court and petitioned that the said Agnes might take a husband if she liked and might then continue apprenticeship or be released on payment of four marks, according as she wished.[9] Usually apprentices took solemn oath not to get married, frequent taverns, tell their master's secrets or rob him of more than six pence a year during term.

Women thus apprenticed could support themselves by their craft if they remained unmarried, or *femmes soles* as they were designated. But it is an interesting fact that there were not only many single women thus engaged in trade, but that many married women went on with their own jobs after marriage and carried on a trade separate from their husbands. Regulations of many medieval towns provide for treatment of wife as a single woman in such cases. When she becomes involved in a trade dispute she is not 'covered' by her husband, i.e. he cannot be made responsible for her debts as he would otherwise be. This was for example the Lincoln rule:

> If any woman that has a husband use any craft within the city, whereof her husband meddles not, she shall be charged as a sole woman as touching such things as belongeth to her craft. And if a plaint be taken against such a woman, she shall answer and plead as a sole woman and make her law and take other advantage in court by plea or otherwise for her discharge. And if she be condemned she shall be committed to prison till she be agreed with the plaintiff, and on goods or chattels that belongeth to husb. shall be confiscated.

We find similar rules in London and a large number of other towns. They were intended for the protection of husbands but none the less represented a notable advance in the position of married women under the common law.

4

Medieval industry was open to women and they played a by no means inconsiderable part in it. There was hardly a craft in which we do not find women. They were butchers, chandlers, ironmongers, net-makers, shoe-makers, glovers, girdlers, haberdashers, purse-makers, cap-makers, skinners, bookbinders, gilders, painters, silk-weavers and embroiderers, spicers, smiths and goldsmiths among many other trades.

This spread of occupations in which women were engaged raises an interesting question. What was the attitude of men towards the co-operation or competition of female labour; and what in particular was the position occupied by women in the predominantly male craft gilds?

We have seen men working side by side with women in many industries, but there are traces of jealousy of the competition of female labour (other than that of the wife or daughter of a craftsman). Thus the London Girdlers enacted in 1344 that no man of the trade should set any woman to work other than his wife or daughter. The Lincoln Fullers ordered in 1297 that 'no one of craft shall work at wooden bar with a woman unless with wife of master or her handmaid'.[10] A complaint made at Bristol in 1461 that weavers set to work or hired to others their wives, daughters and maidens, 'by the which many & divers of the King's liege people, likely men to do the king service in his wars and defence of this land and sufficiently learned in the said craft goeth vagrant and unoccupied and may not have their labour to their living', and weavers were forbidden to employ women except those then getting their livelihood thus.[11]

The reason occasionally given for barring employment of women was that work of a particular craft was too hard for them, but the main reason was the same as that which animates hostility to female labour today. Women's wages were lower even for the same work, and men were afraid of being undercut by cheap labour.

About the position occupied by women in medieval craft gilds it is difficult to generalise. We find women members of social and religious gilds which were commonly associated with crafts and, as wives and daughters of craftsmen, they will be found taking part in social and religious functions connected with craft gilds. Yet in a few crafts we find women explicitly mentioned as members among male masters, for example, in the craft gilds of barber-surgeons of York and London and the dyers of Bristol. But it may well be that these were widows. By an old London custom widows of London freemen were recognised as freewomen of the city. From this it can be deduced that they were able to carry on their husbands' trades as members of their craft gilds, or as if they were members. London records contain numerous references to male apprentices who, on the death of their masters, continued to serve with their widows and even engaged themselves anew to widows of masters. There are hardly any references in London records to women who are not widows admitted to the freedom of the City, and *eo ipso* to the membership of a gild, but that such women existed is shown by the regulation that *femmes couvertes*, practising crafts by themselves, could take women apprentices. Indeed, references to gild apprentices and women masters in the London records are quite numerous, and ordinances of several companies – saddlers, smiths, pewterers – mention 'sisters' of the craft, though it is quite possible that these women were wives or widows of 'brothers' and shared only in the social activities of the gilds.[12]

Thus the general impression is that women were rarely admitted as full members to English craft gilds. Even in trades exclusively in the hands of women there is no evidence of their recognition as a craft. This is especially remarkable in the case of the silk industry. The industry was almost entirely in the hands of women, and wives of better class citizens of London specialised in it. These silkwomen took apprentices and registered their indentures in the usual way. They were sufficiently conscious of common interests to petition the Crown in 1368 and again in 1455 against the competition of alien men, Lombards in particular.

> Sheweth unto your great wisdoms and also prayen and beseechen the Silkwomen and Throwstres of the Crafts and occupation of silkwork w'in the City of London, which be and have been crafts of women w'in the same city of time that no mind runneth to the contrary – That where upon the same crafts, before this time, many a worshipful woman within the city have lived full honourably and therewith many good households kept and many gentlewomen and others in great number like as there be more than 1000, have been drawn under them in learning the same crafts and occupation full virtuously under the plesaunce of God, whereby afterwards they have grown to great worship . . .[13]

Yet there is no trace of a gild of silkwomen. The only instance of anything remotely approaching a gild of women workers so far brought to light is in orders issued in Southampton 1503 for the regulation of packing of wool for loading on to ships, which seems to have been done by women. Women were to choose two of their number annually to be wardens of their company, vacancies in the company were to be filled by nomination of Mayor and Corporation, and women were to 'work the balons and pokes with their own hands and not to bawl nor scold one with another'.

The want of recognition in women's industries in England is the more striking when we contrast it with the situation in France at practically the same date. The famous *Book of Crafts* of Etienne Boileau drawn up in the last half of the thirteenth century contains a schedule of 100 crafts practised in the city of Paris. Of these at least five were in the hands of craftswomen alone, and in a large number of others women were employed as well as men. Crafts monopolised by women were organised on exactly the same basis as those carried on by men, and in crafts shared between men and women, women entered on the same terms as men and were subject to the same regulations.[14]

From the point of view of women, even more important than regular shopkeeping crafts were what we may call bye industries carried on in the home. These were followed by the majority of women workers and spread all over the countryside as well as in towns. They fall into two great classes: those connected with the textile industries and those connected with the production or sale of food and drink. Whereas men as a rule confined themselves to a single craft, it is not uncommon to find women following two or three bye industries of this sort. It is indeed possible that the practice of duplicating crafts and working for a supplementary wage may be one of the reasons which militated against the organisation of women in gilds, even in proper shopkeeping crafts. It would obviously have been impossible for Rose the Regrater, wife of Avarice in *Piers Plowman*, to have been simultaneously under the jurisdiction of two gilds:

> My wife was a weaver and woollen cloth made
> She spake to the spinners to spinnen it out
> ... I bought her barley malt, she brew it to sell
> ... Rose the Regrater was her right name
> She hath holden huckstery all her life time[15]

In other words she not only carried on business as weaver and brewer (both of which were organised craft gilds) but also as huckster or retailer of food and drink.

Assize rolls and other judicial records relating to the enforcement of statutes of labourers cite very large numbers of women not only doing agricultural labour, or employed as spinners and weavers or alewives, but also retailing corn for sale, making and selling charcoal.[16] Such a combination of occupations was common in country districts, and it is obvious that where women brewed ale and practised textile or other crafts as bye employment, and coupled it with their ordinary wage work or with occasional sales of

26 *Silk women. Collecting cocoons and weaving cloth*

market produce, there was some reason for the fact that they were not organised in gilds. This view is upheld by a statute of 1363 which ordains that
every male artificer was to choose his trade and then to confine himself to
that trade alone and constantly.

But the intent of the King and his Council is that Women, that is to say

27 *Attending to the wine*

Brewers, Bakers, Carders, Spinners and Workers as well of Wool as of Linen Cloth and of Silk, Brawdesters and Breakers of Wool and all other that do use and work all handy works may freely use and work as they have done before this time without any impeachment or being restrained by this Ordinance.[17]

Nevertheless the fact that many women's handicrafts were bye industries

56

and were practised in combination will not explain the absence from craft gilds of regular traders, carrying on business as *femmes soles* with regular male and female apprentices. Nor does it explain the fact that spinning, practised to a great extent as a bye industry both in France and in England and in both countries practised almost exclusively by women, was organised in a gild in Paris and not in England.

These bye industries require further attention if only because they constituted in many ways the most important contribution of women to the economic life of the nation, apart from home-making. All spinning and silk-making, some of the weaving and a great deal of brewing of medieval England was in the hands of women, and many women followed these trades with a regularity sufficiently professional to earn for themselves the title of spinster, webster, brewster, in official documents such as Poll Taxes or Subsidy Rolls.

Thus the Poll Tax returns for the West Riding of Yorkshire dating to the last quarter of the fourteenth century give a very good idea of industrial occupations of women in a country district.[18] The returns will not yield exact statistical measurements since names and surnames sometimes do and sometimes do not denote a person's occupation. By the end of the fifteenth century surnames still often were personal and descriptive of occupation or appearance or home of an individual, but they were often handed on from father to son and husband to wife as today, and are not therefore a safe guide. But if we take only the cases in which occupations are specifically given, we note 6 chapmen or pedlars (besides many more with ambiguous surnames which may denote occupation), 39 brewsters, 11 innkeepers, 2 farmers, 1 farrier, 1 smith, 1 shoe-maker, 1 merchant, 2 nurses and 114 domestic or farm servants. Excluding the latter, the most numerous occupations are those connected with the cloth trade. There are 66 websters (weavers) besides 30 with that surname, 2 'listers' or dyers and many more with the feminine form of the term (lystster) for a surname, 2 fullers and many with the surname of fuller. It is remarkable that in this roll not a single woman seems to be described as 'spinster' although that industry was entirely in the hands of women and large numbers must have practised it. Where surnames have female terminations, e.g. bakester, kemster, and lauender or laundress and possibly in the case of fisher, flesher, net-maker and mustard-maker, they almost certainly indicate occupations.

Where Poll Tax rolls group households together the cases when a woman is supplementing her husband's wage by bye industry of her own can be

28 *The fishmonger's shop*

plainly seen. In one of the Suffolk returns such cases come out very clearly. Here is one example.

John Wroo, shepherd
Agneta his wife, webster
Margery his daughter, webster
Thomas, his servant
Beatrice, his servant[19]

Of the two main bye industries, that of cloth remained one of the chief occupations of women until it passed into factories at the end of the eighteenth century. The two chief localities were East Anglia and the West of England. Here by the second half of the fourteenth century there had already appeared big capitalist clothiers who organised the industry and sent great bales of cloth to London and the ports to be exported all over Europe. We find women employed in almost all the stages of cloth production, not only in England but in cloth districts of the Netherlands, Northern France and Italy. We find them among the big clothiers, like Chaucer's Wife of Bath:

> Of cloth making she hadded suich an haunt
> She passed them of Ypres and of Gaunt.

Women performed nearly all the preliminary processes, e.g. combing and carding wool. The spinning of yarn was entirely in their hands. Does the Wife of Bath not remark that God's gifts to women are 'deceit, weeping and spinning'? The craft was practised largely by single women and supplied so many of them with a means of livelihood that the term spinster became synonymous with a single woman; and we still speak of the distaff side of the family when we mean the mother's side. As it took about five spinners to keep one weaver going, the industry kept women employed far outside its own localities and clothiers in East Anglia and the West had to import yarn from other places. Weaving was most commonly done by men, although women were also engaged in it. The Yorkshire cloth district was not yet as important in the Middle Ages as it was to become later. There the organisation of industry was rather different – no big clothiers, but small men working with the help of their wives and families and a few journeymen and taking their pieces of cloth on horseback to market every week.

It has already been mentioned here that women also took part in large numbers of trades connected with making and purveying of food. Brewing, for instance, was largely, though not exclusively, in the hands of women and was a favourite occupation for married women. Information about them is chiefly obtained from records of continual breach of the Assize of Ale. It is rare to find a record of any session of a borough or manor court in which brewsters were not fined for using false measures or for buying and selling contrary to assize. In the last years of the fourteenth century large numbers of brewsters were prosecuted under the Statute of Labourers for demanding excessive payment.

Bread-making was also an occupation carried on by women, although it seems in most cases to have been men's work. It was largely a town craft: in London and other large towns bakeresses or baxters were very numerous. Like brewsters they sold their wares either retail or wholesale, and like them they were often prosecuted under the Assize of Bread and Ale. And it is not uncommon to find a woman doubling the two crafts.

Among trades followed by women there was a number of other occupations, e.g. selling in markets, which from the fact they had no connection

29 *Wool: shearing and weaving*

with gilds were regarded essentially as women's occupations. Regraters or
hucksters (i.e. retailers) were often women. They sold bread, ale, fish,
poultry and all manner of eatables. We find a Nottingham jury presenting
that all hucksters of Nottingham sold garlic, flour, salt, tallow candles, butter,
cheeses and suchlike commodities very dearly and that all of them made
candles without wicks to the deception of the people.[20] Gower in his *Mirour
de l'Omme* has a malicious passage about them. After describing the trickery
of the male regrater he continues:

> But to say the truth in this instance the trade of regratery belongeth by
> right the rather to women. But if a woman be at it she in her stinginess
> useth much more machination and deceit than a man; for never alloweth
> she the profit on a single crumb to escape her, nor faileth to hold her
> neighbour to paying his price. All who beseech her do but lose their
> time, for nothing doth she by courtesy, as anyone who drinketh in her
> house knoweth full well.[21]

Trade in food was also carried on by innkeepers, called in the Middle

30 *Cooking*

Ages typelers, gannokers, hostelers or tapsters. Sometimes women are found managing large establishments. Then as now inns served the twofold purpose of a resting place for travellers to pass the night and a meeting place for inhabitants of the village to foregather for a drink and a gossip. Women were almost as good customers as they were taverners. A racy description of the society which was to be met at the country inns will be found in Langland's famous description of the tavern kept by Beton the Brewster, who tempted Glutton in on his way to holy church; or Skelton's equally racy tale of the tunning of Eleanor Rumming.

61

31 *Women harvesting*

5

Much less prominent in medieval sources, perhaps because it was taken for granted, was the largest class of working women, peasants and dwellers on all manors scattered up and down England. Most of them were expected, if they were married, to share in all their husband's labours on their family holdings. In addition they were burdened with chores which were traditionally feminine. The keeping of the house was of course one of them, the making of cloths and clothes (both for own use and for sale) was another. When Helmbrecht, an ambitious peasant hero of the famous German poem of the same name, tries to persuade his sister Gotelinde to flee the house of her peasant parents and marry a man who would enable her to lead the life of a lady, he reminds her of what her existence would otherwise be. 'You will never be more wretched than if you marry a peasant. You will be compelled to spin, to scour the flax, to comb the hemp, wash and wring clothes, dig up the beets.' Helmbrecht's list of the tasks which life imposed on a peasant wife was of course too short. For instance, it says nothing of the strenuous hours and weeks which a working wife was called upon to spend by her husband's side in fields and pastures.[22]

These tasks weighed no less, often even more, on women who, whether married or not, possessed holdings in their own names – mostly widows, or unmarried women. This was perhaps the most hardworked class of all. In every manorial survey one will find a certain number of women as free tenants, villeins or cotters, holding their virgate of few acres like men and liable to pay the same services for them – so many days' labour a week perhaps, so many boon services at sowing or harvest, so many cartings, so many eggs or pullets or pence per year. No doubt they hired men for heavy ploughing but probably performed other services in person.

We find in manorial accounts women hired by the bailiff to do all sorts of agricultural labour. In fact there was hardly any work except ploughing for which they were not engaged, e.g. planting peas and beans, weeding, reaping, binding, threshing, winnowing, thatching. They did much of the sheep shearing. One of the most important of regular servants of the manor was the dairy woman or *daye* who looked after dairy and poultry on the manor farm. A charming picture of a *daye* drawn by Chaucer at the beginning of the *Nun's Priest's Tale*:

A poore widow, somedeal steep in age
Was whildom dwelling in a narrow cottage
Beside a grove, standing in a dale
This widow, of which I telle you my tale
Since thilke day that she was last a wife
In patience ledde a full simple life.
For little was her chattel and her rent.
By husbandry, of such as God her sent
She found herself and eke her daughters two
Three large sowes had she and namo,
Three kine and eek a sheep that hight Malle
Full sooty was her bower and eke her hall,
In which she ate full many a slender meal.
Of poignant sauce her needed never a deal.
No dainty morsel passed through her throat.
Her diet was according to her coat.
Repletion ne mede her never sick,
A temperate diet was all her physik,
And exercise and heartes suffisaunce,
The goute let her nothing for to daunce,
Nor appoplexy shente not her head;
No wine drank she neither white nor red,
Her board was served most with white and black
Milk and brown bread, in which she found no lack,
Seynd bacon and sometimes an egg or tweye,
And she was as it were a manes deye.

Chaucer depicts a simple and frugal but not an uncomfortable existence. But life for these women of the soil must often have been a hard one. A serio–comic picture of the trials of a country labourer's wife is given in a treatise called *Holy Maidenhead*, in which the author tries to persuade girls to become nuns by drawing a most gloomy picture of married life in all classes of society.

What if I ask besides, that it may seem odious, how the wife stands, that heareth when she cometh in her child scream, sees the cat at the flitch and the hound at the hide, – her cake is burning on the stone hearth and her calf is sucking all the milk up, the earthen pot is running into the fire and the churl is scolding. Tho' it is an odious tale it ought, maidens, to

32 *Haymaking*

deter thee the more strongly from marriage, for it seems not easy to her that trieth it.[23]

Langland paints a truer and more tragic picture of life of women who live

in cottages, their unending labour and brave face turned to the world. He
calls them:

> Poor folk in cotes
> Charged with children and chief lordës rent;
> What they with spinning may spare, spend they it
> in house hire,
> Both in milk and in meal to make therewith
> Papelots (porridge)
> To glut therewith their children that cry after food.
> Also themselves suffer much hunger
> And woe in winter time, with waking a-nights
> To rise to the [bedside] to rock the cradle . . .
> Both to card and to comb, to clout and to wash
> To rub and to reel and rushes to peel,
> That ruth is to read or in rime to show
> The woe of those women that woneth in cots.[24]

Elsewhere he gives a poignant description of her and her husband – poor
and wretched folk – at work in the fields.

> His coat of the cloth that is named carry-marry
> His hood full of holes with the hair sticking through them
> His clumsy knobbed shoes cobbled over so thickly
> Though his toes started out as he trod on the ground,
> His hose hanging over each side of his hoggers,
> All plashed in the puddles as he followed the plow,
> Two miserable mittens made out of old rags,
> The fingers worn out and the filth clotted on them,
> He wading in mud, almost up to his ankles,
> And before him four oxen, so weary and feeble,
> One could reckon their ribs, so rueful were they.
> His wife walked beside him, with a long ox goad,
> In a clouted coat cut short to the knee,
> Wrapped in a winnowing sheet to keep out the weather.[25]

Such compensations as this life had – and it had some – were not all
manorial. The village society was advancing steadily in freedom in Western
Europe during the Middle Ages, and harsh and coarse and laborious as it
was, peasant women's life had its rude gaieties and there may often have

33 *By the fire*

been some truth in Christine de Pisan's judgment: 'Albeit they be fed with coarse bread, milk, lard and pottage and drink water, and albeit they have care and labour enow, yet is their life surer, yea, they have greater sufficiency, than some that be of high estate.' Christine could with some justice have added greater equality and perhaps even greater self-respect to the compensating advantages of the peasant woman's existence.

The education of women

1

The education of women in the Middle Ages is not an easy subject to study or to expound. Although some idea of the general training in good manners, housecraft and piety can easily be derived from a variety of sources, it is rather difficult to obtain exact information about the intellectual instruction, save in the case of certain aristocratic ladies and certain nuns. We may perhaps begin our survey by describing the books of deportment and educational treatises addressed to women in the Middle Ages; then proceed to the three types of education open to women, in nunnery schools, in great households, in elementary schools for boys and girls in town and occasionally country, and lastly analyse the existing evidence of the literacy of women in the later Middle Ages.

2

A good deal about women's education can be deduced from the didactic works addressed to them throughout the Middle Ages, especially from the early thirteenth century onwards. These works throw considerable light on medieval ideas about women and their education – taking education in the widest sense as a preparation for life. In this widest sense education comprised the inculcation of good manners, good religion and good housecraft and not merely intellectual instruction, about which medieval books tell us relatively little.

Judged by didactic treatises, the education of women was in the main strictly vocational. The treatises fall into two main classes. The first comprises books and treatises dealing with courtly education. Their object was to fashion ladies who would shine in society. They are therefore largely taken up with rules for playing the game of courtly love, very frivolous in tone and containing minute instructions for the care of person and deportment – many modelled on Ovid's *Art of Love*. Most famous are two long

34 *A lady at chess*

French poems of the thirteenth century by Robert de Blois and Jacques d'Amiens. But it is noticeable that the notion of polished manners required of society ladies included a wide range of what we would now call accomplishments. Hawking, playing chess, telling stories, responding with witty repartee, singing and playing on various musical instruments, were all required; and it was also assumed that ladies would be able to read and write. What these requirements aimed at is demonstrated by the idealised image of ladies in contemporary poetic romances. Robert de Blois in one poem enumerates the qualities of the heroine thus:

35 *Music-making*

She could carry and fly falcon, tercel and hawk,
She knew well how to play chess and tables,
how to read romances, tell tales and
sing songs. All the things a well-bred
lady ought to know she knew and lacked none.[1]

In the romance of *Flamenca* the sorely tried heroine is addressed by one of her maidens thus:

A lady is all the better if she be a little adorned with learning. For indeed you, Madam, tell me, if you hadn't known as much as you do how would you have passed over these two years, during which you have suffered such cruel torments? You would have been dead with grief. But however great your sadness, it disappeared when you read a little. 'Friend' said Flamenca, pressing her in her arms, 'You speak wisely. For no reposte is pleasant to a man who is ignorant of letters and you will ever see that persons who are learned regret that they are not more so.'[2]

36 Christine de Pisan at her study

Thus courtly education envisaged in courtly books of deportment and described in romances is frivolous and is concerned with accomplishments, but is by no means devoid of a certain intellectual quality.

The more serious didactic works on the bringing up of women are different in tone. While the object of the courtly treatise is attracting lovers, these aim at keeping husbands. The training of a good wife is much more serious and of greater pedagogic value, but is also strictly vocational. Some of these treatises such as those of Philippe de Navarre, F. de Barberino and the Knight of La Tour Landry were written for ladies of gentle birth.[3] Others were intended for the bourgeoisie, and of these far the best are *Le*

Menagier de Paris, and the little English poem 'How the Goodwife taught her daughter'. Some, like Christine de Pisan's *Livre des Trois Vertus*, were meant for all classes. All these various treatises concern themselves with the attitude of wife to husband and with religious duties, and devote much attention to instruction in Christian faith and the practice of piety, missing from courtly treatises.

Perhaps the romantic ladies of the courtly treatises and poems alarmed the stout conservatives and moral gentlemen who wrote the serious treatises about bringing up girls. For it is a curious fact that the serious treaties often express doubt whether it is wise to allow any woman except nuns to have learning. Barberino will allow a noble girl to read and write so that she should be able to govern her estates; but he debates whether daughters of ordinary gentlemen ought to be taught, and decides against it; and he forbids outright any learning for daughters of merchants or artisans. Phillippe de Navarre categorically forbids women to read or write, and the Knight of La Tour Landry will allow them only the knowledge of reading, so that women may read scriptures. All of them want to constrict women's minds as Chinese constricted their feet; the reason is the fear of their reading demoralising romances and writing love letters.

It is however clear that these authors were old fashioned, since sensible writers like the Menagier de Paris and Christine de Pisan wished women to read and write. But even these more enlightened treatises give little information as to the extent of intellectual education or method of acquiring it. For our answers to these questions we must turn to other sources.

3

It appears from these other sources that there were several, at least four, different ways in which the women of the Middle Ages were able to acquire literary education: by instruction in schools in nunneries for the gentry and the better class of bourgeoisie; by being sent to the households of great ladies, where they could learn breeding and no doubt acquire some intellectual attainments; by technical and general education provided by apprenticeship or the bourgeois equivalent of the above, available for girls of craftsmen class in towns; by elementary schooling for girls of poorer classes in town and country.

Let us begin with the nunneries. It used to be the common assumption that nunneries were almost solely responsible for the education of girls in the Middle Ages. In truth, the extent to which the practice prevailed is greatly exaggerated. It was fairly general, but as English evidence shows not all nunneries kept schools, and when they did, the schools were seldom large. Perhaps two out of three English nunneries took schoolgirls as boarders, and most of these took only a small number. Some nunneries were themselves often small and poor and could not have looked after any pupils. It is however interesting to observe that nunneries were used not only as girls' schools but as infant schools for boys. We hear of a five-year-old boy sent by saintly Hugh of Lincoln at the close of the twelfth century to Elstow Abbey to learn letters.[4] In 1527 Sir John Stanley provided in his will that his little son and heir was to be brought up by the Abbess of Barking until twelve and then by the Abbot of Westminster. We continually come across references to little boys in reports of episcopal visitations of nunneries.[5]

The size of the nunneries themselves imposed one limit on the number of children who could receive convent education, expenses imposed another. The nuns charged fees for board and tuition, and the fees were high – indeed so high that even parents of gentle birth could sometimes find them too heavy. Some time ago Professor de Montmorency found in the Public Record Office a pathetic petition from the Prioress of the little nunnery of Cornworthy (Devon) to the effect that Laurence Knight, gentleman, had agreed with the late Prioress to take his two daughters, Elizabeth aged seven and Jane aged ten 'to teche them to school' at a fee of 10d. per week each. They accordingly remained there for five years until money due amounted to £21 13s. 4d., not one penny of which was paid. Laurence meanwhile departed this life leaving his wife Jane executrix, and Jane married again and refused to pay. One is uncertain whom to pity most; the Prioress left with this incubus on her hands, or Elizabeth and Jane Knight trying hard to restrain their appetites and not to grow out of their clothes under her justly incensed regard.[6]

What exactly did the nuns teach children? This is a difficult question to answer: difficult because contemporary evidence is scarce, and because the value of education varied greatly from age to age, and also with the intellectual level of the nuns themselves. Generally speaking in the early centuries of the Middle Ages the intellectual standards at many houses were quite high. But in the later centuries the education of the nuns themselves grew progressively worse, and Latin had died out of most convents in the fourteenth century and French in the fifteenth century.

Modern writers have tried to make up for lack of direct evidence by drawing up imaginary curricula, and they grew more and more ambitious as they copied the curricula from each other. In the seventeenth century Aubrey says 'here they learned needlework, art of confectionery, surgery, physic, writing, drawing etc.' But in the work of a writer of the mid-nineteenth century the list becomes 'reading, writing, some knowledge of arithmetic, art of embroidery, music and French of school of Stratford atte Bowe, preparation of perfumes, balsams, simples and confectionery'. Another writer adds a few more touches, 'treatment of various disorders, compounding of simples, binding up of wounds, fancy cookery such as making of sweetmeats, drawing, needlework of all kinds and music both vocal and instrumental'. Students of human nature cannot but smile to see music insinuate itself into the list and become both instrumental and vocal. Confectionery extends itself to include perfumes, balsams, simples and sweetmeats; arithmetic appears out of nowhere, and even dancing trips in on light fantastic toe. In Malory's *Morte d'Arthur*, there is a passage where it is said of Arthur's fairy sister Morgan le Fay, who bewitched Merlin, that 'she was put to school in a nunnery and there she learned so much that she was a great clerk of necromancy'. This would add black magic to the curriculum of nunnery schools!

The sober fact is we have no evidence about what was taught except inferences from what we know of the education of nuns themselves. Latin could not have been taught in the fourteenth century or French in the fifteenth century since nuns themselves did not know these languages in those times. Children were doubtless taught the Credo, the Ave and the Paternoster by rote, and must have been taught to read, although it is more doubtful whether they learned to write. Probably they learned songs with the nuns, and spinning and needlework. Beyond these accomplishments nuns doubtless taught piety and good breeding; and the standard of these, though good in some houses, could not have been very high in others, judging from visitation reports.

If children of gentle birth were not sent to nunneries for education, how otherwise could they receive it? It seems likely that in many cases they were either brought up at home or sent into households of great ladies, to attend on them and to receive training on good breeding. All great fifteenth-century collections of letters from English gentry – Paston Letters, Stonor Papers and Plumpton Correspondence[7] show us girls sent away from home to be in attendance on some mistress of rank. They probably gained a good practical training and (what was equally important for them) were in a position to make good marriages. But this correspondence also seems to show that the girls were often unhappy. It is an odd coincidence that in all these three groups of letters, all the letters speak of the unhappiness felt by the girls in other people's houses. It is possible that they were not treated more severely than they would have been in their own homes. The Middle Ages took a stern view of parental responsibility, and parents exacted rigid respect and obedience and beat both boys and girls assiduously. It will be remembered how the gentle Lady Jane Gray was by her parents 'so sharply taunted, so cruelly threatened, yea presently sometimes with pinches, nips and bobs that I thought myself in hell', and Margaret Paston's treatment of her daughter was by modern standards nothing short of odious.[8]

What intellectual education boys and girls received at home is hard to discover. Sometimes no doubt they learned from a tutor, as gentle (let us hope) as Ascham was to Lady Jane Gray; or from a resident chaplain, such as Gautier de Biblesworth who made a French vocabulary in the fourteenth century for the noble lady Dionysia de Montchensi of Kent. In *romans d'aventure* of the twelfth and thirteenth centuries we invariably encounter noble ladies learning to read. Sometimes even 'school' is spoken of, though whether a nunnery school is meant or a collection of young persons learning breeding in the household, we do not know. What is notable is that boys and girls were taught together. Chronicler Froissart in a poem called 'Espinette Amoureuse' (*c.* 1350) tells us how he went to school to learn Latin when he was twelve, but neglected lessons to give presents of pins and apples to little girls who sat on the bench with him, and how he wondered when the time would come when he would be grown up and could make love to them. Here we apparently find boys and girls together at school and learning Latin. But it is possible that this particular school was a nunnery.[9]

There is no evidence to show that girls ever attended the grammar schools which we know existed for boys; but on the other hand it is clear that some elementary schools were available for both sexes in the towns. At Paris there were the so-called 'little schools' under the government of the Cantor of Notre Dame, which taught reading and the rudiments of Latin grammar, and which catered for girls as well as for boys. The name of one Paris schoolmistress who kept such a school in 1292 is on record. In the following century Paris *scholastici* when summoning assemblies of teachers of 'little schools' included 'women keeping and teaching schools in the art of grammar' and in 1380 twenty-one schoolmistresses registered with masters.

In Germany, too, elementary schools for girls were widespread in towns

37 *Teaching*

in the later Middle Ages. At Emmerich in 1445, a compact was sealed between town and chapter by which the former claimed the right to elect two, or when necessary more, women as teachers for girls and girls' schools; and women teachers are also mentioned in many other German towns.[10]

For England the evidence is more scanty. There is reference in 1404 to a *magistra scholarum* at Boston and since *magister scholarum* is a technical term for a master of a grammar school it seems possible that some girls were learning Latin at Boston at that date. It was in the following year that the famous statute of 1405 laid down that 'every man or woman of whatever state or condition that he be, shall be free to set son or daughter to take learning on any school that pleases them within the realm'.[11]

It is not clear what schools were meant by the statute. Direct evidence for attendance of girls at elementary schools in England is scanty in the extreme, though it seems possible that such schools were sometimes kept by priests. A petition of the end of the fifteenth century shows a girl of seven (a daughter of a London draper) attending a school of thirty children kept by an old priest. Women were also included in the prohibition of Lollard schools in the fifteenth century.[12]

However, in spite of the evidence for the existence of elementary schools in foreign countries and a certain amount of corresponding information for England, elementary education cannot have been widespread. Such elementary schools as there were, doubtless served the petty bourgeoisie of towns, not the country folk or children of the lowest class. Nor is it likely that the curriculum was a wide one. Names of Paris schoolmistresses show them drawn from a class of small shopkeepers. They could not have been much better instructed than the old ladies who kept dame schools of a later age, and probably taught good behaviour rather than learning. The learning probably included the alphabet, catechism and other religious knowledge. In the English priests' school mentioned above children learnt 'Pater Noster, Ave and Credo with further learning', but it is impossible to say what that further learning embraced.

The effectiveness of all these educational provisioners is difficult to judge. What we know about the standards of literacy and intellectual accomplishments of women is largely based on inference. It seems clear both from romances and from certain historical incidents that in the most exalted class ladies were often able to read romances and to judge the merits of a poem. Indeed in the twelfth century it was the great ladies of the Courts of Champagne and Provence, who were the patronesses of troubadours. The education of nuns at this earlier date must also have been good. The thirteenth century was the golden age of the German convent of Helfta whose nuns wrote learned scientific treatises in Latin as well as religious works.[13] Courtly education sometimes produced authoresses like Marie de France, in the thirteenth century, and Christine de Pisan in the fifteenth, who may fairly be called a blue-stocking. In her eloquent plea for the education of women, Christine de Pisan quotes the tale of a professor at one of the Italian universities, who had such a learned daughter that he used sometimes to send her to give his lectures for him. And as she was very beautiful, Christine explains, he hung a little veil before her face, so as not to distract students from learning!

Women in the families of ordinary gentry and bourgeoise seem often to have been able to read. Simple gentlewomen like Pastons and Stonors could read and write, though they were apparently not very handy with the pen and often employed secretaries. In the Plumpton Correspondence of the same period we find one grandfather writing to another 'Your daughter and mine speaketh prettily and French and hath neat hand, and learned her psalter'; and she was only three.

Throughout the fourteenth and fifteenth centuries, wills show women in possession of books, most often psalters and other service books, but sometimes romances and other books as well. Here are two or three examples. In 1269 William de Beauchamp leaves his daughter Joan a book of *Lancelot*; and in 1380 Elisabeth de la Zouche leaves to her husband a book called *Tristrem and Lancelot* and to a certain churchman her portiforium psalter and other books. In 1395 Alice Lady West leaves her daughter-in-law 'all my books of Latin, English and French' and in 1432 the woman servant of a York chaplain receives under a will 'an English book of fables and tales'.

Twenty years later the fortunate niece of Sir Thomas Cumberworth receives by his will 'my book of the tales of Canterbury'. But with the exception of a few women like the chaplain's maidservant most of these recipients were gentlewomen of good family. Books occur more rarely in the wills of lesser persons.[14]

It is a safe guess that the education of women of the upper classes and better bourgeoisie in the later Middle Ages comprised at least reading and writing; no such guess can be made of the education of lower classes. About the latter it is very difficult to say anything at all, except that women of humble rank had a better chance of an education in the town than in the country. We have seen that the technical education of apprenticeship was open to women in towns. Occasionally, they may have got even more than that in the urban elementary schools. Among the humbler townsfolk of East Anglia prosecuted as Lollards in the fifteenth century only a few women were indicted for reading English translations of the Bible.[15] On the other hand it is certain that the overwhelming majority of peasant women or general domestic servants received no education at all. They might be instructed in the rudiments of religion by a parish priest, but it is unlikely that they could read themselves. They were doubtless as illiterate as Jeanne d'Arc, most famous of peasant girls, who knew neither 'a' nor 'b', or as Villon's old mother, for whom he wrote the most touching of all his Ballades 'pour prier nostre Dame'. 'A poor old woman am I, who know nothing. I never learned letters. In my parish church I see Paradise painted with harps and lutes, and hell where the damned are roasted. The one affrights, the other fills me with joy and delight.' The poor woman's Bible was her parish church.[16]

One special branch of knowledge deserved perhaps special discussion. All women were expected to know something of family medicine, and it is noticeable that there existed various treatises on diseases of women specially written or translated for their use, with the plain assumption that they will be able to read. In the fourteenth century an English version of a treatise attributed to Trotula – Dame Trot of the English nursery lore – is prefaced by a translator's explanation that as 'women of our tongue do better read and understand this language than any other, and every woman lettered read it to other unlettered and help them and counsel them in their maladies withouten showing their disease to man, I have this drawn and written in English.[17]

If however a woman set up in practice as a physician outside the limits of her home and pretended to something more than the skill of an amateur, she forthwith provoked an outcry which seems to foreshadow the opposition of

38 *Compounding a potion*

the medical profession to the entrance of women in the nineteenth century. The doctors' case was a respectable one: women had no medical degrees and therefore no knowledge or training. Nevertheless here and there were women who acquired considerable fame as physicians. Trotula and the women doctors of the University of Salerno in the eleventh and twelfth centuries, are mythical figures, rapidly melting away under the cruel searchlight of modern research. But in the early fourteenth century there was a very remarkable woman doctor practising in Paris. Her name was Jacqueline Felicie de Almania and she was described as a noble lady and presumably was German by origin. In 1322, being then about thirty years old, she was prosecuted by the medical faculty of Paris on a charge of contravening the statute which forbade anyone to practise medicine in the city and suburbs without a faculty's decree and the Chancellors' licence. Various witnesses were called to testify to the skill of her diagnosis and treatment, and several of them said they had been given up by various doctors before being cured by her, and set forth names of these legitimate, but unsuccessful doctors. Her skill seems to have been generally accepted. One of the witnesses expressly stated that 'he had heard it said by several that she was wiser in the art of surgery and medicine than the greatest master doctor or surgeon in Paris'. She herself made an eloquent and sensible defence arguing that the statute under which she was arraigned was intended to restrain ignorant and foolish persons who knew not the art of medicine, whereas she was well instructed and skilled therein, as might be seen from her successful cures. She went on to speak of the need for women doctors in general, saying that many women were ashamed to reveal their infirmities to a man and that women had often died sooner than do so. Nevertheless she was prohibited from practising; but as she had already disregarded a previous prohibition and fine, she probably went on as before.[18] Nor was she the only woman practising illicitly in Paris at this time, for one Joanna, called 'lay sister but a married woman', Belota the Jewess and Margaret of Ypres, described as surgeon, were prohibited to practise medicine at the same time, and between 1322 and 1331 several other women were similarly indicted.[19]

Nunneries[1]

I

We must guard ourselves against exaggerating the size and the importance of nunneries in the Middle Ages. In England there were in all between the years 1250 and 1540, between 126 and 136 nunneries, excepting the Gilbertine ones of which there were 10. Among them were some great and famous abbeys, e.g. Barking in Essex, the Wessex houses of Romsey, Wherwell, St Mary's Winchester, Wilton, Shaftesbury ('If the Abbot of Glastonbury could marry the Abbess of Shaftesbury, their heir would have more land than the King of England'). All these rich old houses were south of the Thames.

The largest number of English nunneries was to be found in the North, the East, and the East Midlands, but they were almost all small and, as a rule, very poor, ranking not as abbeys but as priories. If we make a rough analysis of the number of inmates at different periods during the fourteenth and the fifteenth centuries we find that, out of 111 houses for which an estimate is possible, only 4 had over 30 inmates, 8 had 20 to 30 inmates, 36 had between 10 and 20 inmates and 63 had fewer than 10. During this period (c. 1350) there cannot have been more than 3500 nuns altogether in England, and these numbers were steadily decreasing to 1900 in 1534.[2]

Nuns were recruited from a limited class. They provided a career for girls of gentle birth for whom the only alternative was marriage. Prioresses of even some of the smallest and poorest houses were drawn from well-known noble and gentry families. The evidence of medieval wills shows how useful nunneries could be to an upper-class family, with several sons to put into the world and daughters to dower. In the course of the Middle Ages wealthy townsmen, often connected by blood with the gentry, sent their daughters to convents in large towns like London and Norwich. But we never find poor girls of lower classes as nuns, because families of these classes needed no special outlets for their women. This was partly because women of working classes in fact worked in agriculture and industry, and partly because families of peasants and artisans could not afford the dowry required to get into a nunnery.

Medieval nunneries, thus recruited, performed a number of functions, and served the women in them in a variety of ways. Certainly some girls went in with no particular aptitude for religious life, and simply because there was nothing else for them to do. But there were also others who found in the monastic environment their full spiritual fulfilment, and in doing so performed a function which rated very high in medieval estimation. Prayer and praise of God was a mode of life to which the Middle Ages attached the greatest importance, and for which monasteries served as the best, perhaps the only, venue. They provided the environment necessary for whole-life and whole-time service of the monastic ideal; and in some places and at some times the nuns so serving could attain a degree of dedication and personal perfection which earned for them a renown in their lifetime and veneration by posterity. One such nun, Euphemia of Wherwell, who excelled in practical virtues, forms the subject of a brief biographical sketch – in fact a panegyric; another English nun – or rather an anchoress connected with Carrow priory – was Julian of Norwich, an outstanding mystical writer of the Middle Ages. Abroad, more particularly in Germany, the ecclesiastical literature preserved the names and the fame of many such women. The life-stories of St Christina of Stommela, or of the three women who made the reputation of the nunnery at Helfta in the thirteenth century – Mechtild of Magdeburg, Mechtild of Hackeborn and Gertrud the Great – were recorded in their autobiographies or near-contemporary biographies. We also possess the evidence of the 'lives' and letters of such great non-German nuns as Liutgard of Tongern, St Claire, St Agnes of Bohemia, or St Douceline, the founding mother of the Béguines of Marseilles.[3] But numerous nuns of smaller stature and less renown also found in their nunneries the *ambiance* for good life and spiritual experience they could not have found outside.

In addition to these spiritual facilities for the best in their ranks, nunneries offered to the main body of nuns opportunities for education, organisation and responsibility, not easy for women to find elsewhere. In the later Middle Ages nunneries may not have always made the best use of these opportunities, but in general, even at this late time, they provided women with openings to a profession and a career.

A further function was to serve as boarding houses for better-off wives and widows. It was obviously convenient for gentlemen to have somewhere to send wives and daughters during a temporary absence, if for some reason they did not want to leave them at home. Sometimes also a widow would go off to a nunnery to end her days in honourable retirement as a boarder. Occasionally these visitors brought gentlewomen companions and maids with them and were a great distraction to the nuns, who saw and imitated their gay clothes and pet dogs, and were willing to gossip with them. Bishops greatly disapproved of boarders and were always trying to turn them out, but never succeeded, because nuns were always hard up and wanted the boarders' fees.

Some nunneries fulfilled yet another function for the upper classes, that of select boarding schools for children. It used to be a common assumption that nunneries were almost solely responsible for the education of children – mainly girls – in the Middle Ages. This assumption, as we have seen, is much too sweeping. By no means all English nunneries kept schools, and when they did, the schools were by no means large. The educational provision nunneries supplied, considered *in toto*, could not have been very great. Moreover it was wholly restricted to children of the upper classes – nobility, gentry and the wealthy merchants.

However, the nunneries also fulfilled certain functions for the lower classes. They may not have received their daughters as nuns, though many convents had 'lay sisters' (*conversae*), but they acted to the best of their ability as centres of almsgiving (though they were becoming lax in this and were often too poor themselves to do much), and played an important part as landlords and employers. They owned home-farms like any other lord of the manor and sometimes possessed large estates. Besides a regular staff of women servants and labourers they would employ a number of thatchers, builders, carpenters from the neighbourhood, and spinners, tailors and other craftsmen to make their clothes. Thus many men and women were dependent on the nunneries as landowners or employers. This role of the nunneries went further than any imagined reverence for their religious calling to explain the anxiety shown in some districts to preserve them when Dissolution came in the sixteenth century.

2

The daily life in a nunnery was conducted according to strict routine. Most monastery rules derived from the Benedictines and were accordingly so planned as to give a religious and carefully ordered existence combining

39 *Nuns in the refectory*

regularity with variety and maintaining a careful balance of prayer, study and labour.

A nun had seven monastic offices or services to say daily. She rose at 2 a.m., went down to choir for Matins, followed by Lauds, returned to bed at dawn and slept for three hours. She got up for the day at 6 a.m. and said Prime. Tierce, Sext, None, Vespers and Compline followed at intervals through the day; the last at 7 p.m. in winter and 8 p.m. in summer, after which she was supposed to go straight to bed. All in all she got about eight hours' sleep broken in the middle by the night service. She had three meals – a light repast of bread and ale after prime in the morning, a solid dinner to accompany reading aloud at midday and a short supper after vespers. From 12 to 5 in winter or 1 to 6 in summer nuns were supposed to devote themselves to work of some kind (digging, haymaking, embroidering, reading) interspersed with a certain amount of sober recreation.

Except for certain periods of relaxation, strict silence had to be observed, and if nuns had to communicate with each other they had to do this by a sort of deaf and dumb language. The persons who drew up the signs in use seem to have combined preternatural ingenuity with a very exiguous sense of humour; the speechless pandemonium which went on at convent dinner must have been more mirth-provoking than speech. A sister who wanted fish would 'wag her hands displayed sidelings in the manner of a fish tail'; if she wanted to say 'pass the milk' she would 'draw her little finger in the manner of milking'; a guilty sacristan struck by the thought that she had not provided incense for mass would 'put her two fingers into her nostrils'.[4]

The existence of the individual nuns was of course closely integrated with the organisation of the community of nuns as a whole. Every monastic house may be considered from two points of view – as a religious unit and a social one. From the religious point of view it was a house of prayer, and its *raison d'être* was the daily round of offices. From the social point of view it was a community of human beings who had to be fed and clothed, which maintained a household of servants, ran a farm, looked after estates, bought and sold and kept accounts. A nun must perforce combine the functions of Martha and Mary, and be no less a housewife than her neighbour, the lady of the manor.

The daily business was in the hands of a number of officials called *obedientiaries* chosen among the most experienced inmates. The most important of them were the Sacristan, who had the charge of the church fabrics and lighting of the house, the Chambresses who looked after the nuns' clothes, and the Cellaress who looked after food and servants, saw to repairs and superintended the home-farm. The details of the nuns' housekeeping can often be had from account rolls, such as the Cellaress's accounts of Syon or the instructions on housekeeping in the Barking Abbey 'Charter'.[5]

40 *Nuns in choir*

In every nunnery the home-farm could provide the greater part of the
bread, meat, beer, vegetables and dairy produce. Anything else had to be
bought, especially three important articles of consumption, fish, salt and
spices, of which nuns consumed a lot.

The chief food in Lent was salt or dried fish and pease pottage, enlivened
with almonds, raisins and figs. At other times of the year there was fresh
or salt fish on fish days, and beef, pork or bacon (more rarely mutton) on
meat days. Fowls were served on festive occasions. In addition there was an
everyday allowance of bread and ale.

The household staff varied with the size of the nunnery. Wages were
paid to a priest, or a chaplain, and a bailiff, the latter an invaluable factotum
and general manager. The larger convents employed a male cook, a brewer,
a baker, a dairywoman, a laundress, a porter and one or more maidservants.
The rule of St Benedict originally contemplated the performance of a good
deal of domestic work by the nuns themselves, but it was largely discarded
by the thirteenth century. If nuns of small convents had to do their own
cooking and housework this was due to poverty and usually drew com-

41 *Nunnery officials. In the top row behind the priests, the sacristan pulls the bell ropes, the abbess holds her crozier and the cellaress her keys. In the bottom row the nuns walk in procession, singing*

plaints from the nuns. In some of the larger houses individual nuns even had private servants.

In the history of medieval nunneries nothing is more striking than the constant financial straits to which they were reduced. There was hardly a house that was not at some period of its career an object of appeal on account of poverty. In smaller and poorer houses nuns seem actually to have gone short of food, and bishops on visitation sometimes remarked with their own eyes holes in the nuns' clothes. We often hear of buildings in ruin or roofs letting in rain. A large proportion of nunneries were chronically in debt.

The poverty was due to many causes. Many convents were insufficiently endowed from the start. They often suffered damage by fire and flood which they found difficult to make good. Nunneries in the north of England suffered from the raids of the Scots and from the general lawlessness which had bad effects on the moral conditions as well as on the financial state of Yorkshire houses. Nunneries also complained of demands for hospitality or pensions by powerful persons whom they could not refuse. Nunneries could also suffer from the incompetence of the nuns themselves. Their functionaries were sometimes extravagant; very frequently they were bad business women. When in need of ready money they often raised it by improvident devices, e.g. by selling woods, leasing farms for long periods at low rent, by promising annual pensions for a lump sum down, by mortgaging land, pawning plate, or running into debt.

In the later Middle Ages nunneries also showed signs of decline in their intellectual standards and moral conditions. In the course of its history monasticism produced many learned nuns, and from time to time certain convents acquired fame for their scholarship. But in England in the later Middle Ages the standard of education was low and learning was on the wane. The decline of learning affected monks as well as nuns, but it went further in nunneries than in monasteries. The decline is evidenced by the very language in which bishops were wont to address injunctions to convents. All through the Middle Ages injunctions to monks were in Latin, but already in the fourteenth century we find bishops writing to nuns in French, because Latin would not be understood, and in the fifteenth century even the knowledge of French dies out of nunneries, and the injunctions are in English. Sometimes nuns and abbesses could not read their own foundation charters. There were several translations of the Rule of St Benedict and of religious books made for the use of nuns in the fifteenth century. It is clear that the knowledge of Latin had by then died out even in the best houses,

42 *A nun in her cell*

though most nuns were no doubt able to read English books of devotion.

Internal discipline also decayed in the later centuries. Increasing laxity showed itself in a variety of directions. One of the first was slackness in the performance of religious duties. A carelessness in singing the monastic hours was a very common fault during the later Middle Ages. With the tradition of learning almost dead, and servants performing most manual labour, monastic life had lost the essential variety which St Benedict had designed for it. As a result, the regularity of daily life sometimes became irksome and a series of services occasionally degenerated into mere routine of peculiar monotony. In this respect monks could be worse than nuns. They sometimes cut services; and sometimes behaved with the utmost levity (e.g. canons of Exeter in 1330 giggled and joked and quarrelled during services and dropped hot candle wax from the upper stalls on to the shaven heads of singers in the stalls below). In the nunneries the visiting bishops noted a tendency to come late (especially to matins in the small hours) and to slip out before the end of the service on any good or bad excuse. But the most common fault was to gabble through the services as quickly as possible in order to get them over. Syllables were left out at the beginning and end of words, dipsalma were omitted so that one side of the choir began the second half before the other side had finished the first half. Sentences were mumbled and slurred. What should have been 'entuned in their nose ful seemily' became a terrible mess of stately plainsong.

The increasing frivolity and worldliness are shown in Chaucer's portrait of Madame Eglentyne as well as in reports of the episcopal visitations. To modern and unmonastic ideas some of the ways in which the frivolity manifested itself seem harmless, but it certainly was subversive of discipline. The bishops were especially shocked to find nuns still retaining the vanities of their sex. The three D's (dances, dresses, dogs) drew special condemnation. The Church reprobated dancing at the best of times and especially in nunneries. Yet in spite of this the account rolls of expenses of medieval nunneries contain payments for wassails at New Year and Twelfth Night, Mayday games, bonfire nights, harpers and players at Christmas and so on; and when we look in bishops' registers we find nuns forbidden 'all manner of ministrelsy, interludes, dancing and revelling'.

Perennially recurring was the question of fashionable dresses. Not for nothing Chaucer remarks how well pinched was Madame Elgentyne's wimple, how elegant her cloaks, how fine her coral rosary and gold brooch. For more than six centuries the bishops waged holy war against fashion in the cloister and waged it in vain. Occasionally a wretched bishop flounders unhandily in masculine bewilderment through something like a complete catalogue of contemporary fashions in order to specify what nuns were not to wear. Synods sat, archbishops and bishops shook their heads over golden hairpins and silver belts, jewelled rings, laced shoes, slashed tunics, low-necked dresses, long trains, gay colours, costly materials and furs.

Dress was merely one way of aping the fashions of the world. Pet animals was another. Bishops regarded pets as bad for discipline and for century after century tried to turn animals out of convents without the least success. Nuns just waited till the bishop went and whistled the dogs back again. Dogs were easily the favourite pets, but nuns also kept monkeys, squirrels, rabbits and birds. They sometimes took animals to church with them.

All these wordly habits were due to another increasing tendency with which the authorities struggled in vain, viz. contact between nuns and seculars. Boarders and friends came in; nuns wandered about outside, 'fish out of water'. Bishops continually attempted to keep nuns shut up. The most strenuous attempts began in 1300 when Pope Boniface VIII published the

Bull *Periculoso*, ordering nuns never, save in exceptional circumstances, to leave convents nor to allow secular persons to visit them without special licence. But no one ever succeeded in putting the Bull in force. At one nunnery in the diocese of Lincoln, when the bishop came to read the Bull and deposited a copy in the house, the nuns pursued him to the gate when he was riding away and threw the Bull at his head.[6] More practical bishops soon stopped trying to enforce the Bull as it stood and contented themselves with ordering nuns not to go out or pay visits too often, or without a companion, or without licence, or without good reason. But nuns went out just the same. What are we to think of the giddy lady 'who on Monday did pass night with Austin friars at N'hampton and did dance and play lute with them in same place till midnight and on night following passed night with Friars Preachers at N'hampton, luting and dancing in like manner'.[7]

To us these frivolities may seem harmless and amiable enough. But we must remember that worse things sometimes followed them. With the majority of English nunneries during the later Middle Ages, nothing more happened than an increasing worldliness. But with some others it was different. Bishops sometimes found nunneries so thoroughly disorderly and immoral that reprimand seemed hopeless.

Undoubtedly the nunneries were decaying when the sixteenth-century Dissolution came upon them. However that may be, it is impossible to deny that throughout their career, even in the period of decline, nunneries were a boon for women of the Middle Ages. To unmarried gentlewomen they gave scope for abilities which might otherwise have run to waste, assuring them both self-respect and the respect of society. They made use of their powers of organisation in the government of communities and in the management of households and estates. They allowed nuns the possibility of a good education (even though its standard declined) and opened up for them when they were capable of rising to such heights, the supreme experiences of contemplative life. Of these potentialities the more notable monastic housewives have left ample record to testify. Even if they suffered decay, and sheltered the idle with the industrious, and black sheep with white, the nunneries still represented an honourable profession and fulfilled a useful function for gentlewomen of the Middle Ages.

Notes

CHAPTER I

1 'Le Vallet aux douze femmes' and 'La Femme que servait cent cavaliers' are typical examples of anti-feminist *fabliaux*. For *fabliaux* in general see *Le Recueil général et complet des fabliaux etc.*, 6 vols., ed. A. de Montaiglon and G. Reynaud, Paris, 1872–90; J. Bédier, *Les Fabliaux*, 5th ed., Paris, 1928 and Per Nykrog, *Les Fabliaux*, Copenhagen, 1957; cf. also J. Bédier, 'Les Fabliaux' in *Histoire de la langue et de la littérature française*, ed. Petit de Tulleville, Paris, 1896, t. II, pp. 89–90.

2 Marie-Josèphe Pinet, *Christine de Pisan, 1364–1430*, Paris, 1927. *Oeuvres Poétiques de Christine de Pisan*, ed. Maurice Roy, Société des Anciens Textes Français, 3 vols., Paris, 1880–95, though confined to Christine's poetic works contains the text of *Epistre au dieu d'amours*: her principal feminist apologia. Cf. a brief sketch in M. Petit de Tulleville's 'Les derniers Poètes du Moyen Age' in *Histoire de la langue et de la littérature française*, ed. Petit de Tulleville, Paris, 1896, t. II, pp. 89–90; J. Nyss, *Christine de Pisan et ses principales oeuvres*, Brussels, 1914; R. Rigaud, *Les Idées feministes de Christine de Pisan*, Neufchâtel, 1911.

3 E.g. nos. 62, 67, 70, 71, in *Die Exempla . . . des Jakob von Vitry*, ed. Joseph Greven, Sammlung den mittelälterlichen Texte, no. 9, Heidelberg, 1914.

4 Cited in E. E. Power, 'The Position of Women' in C. G. Crump and E. F. Jacob (ed.), *The Legacy of the Middle Ages*, Oxford, 1926, p. 402.

5 E. E. Power (ed.), *The Goodman of Paris*, London, 1928. 'The Clerk's Tale', *Canterbury Tales*, in Geoffrey Chaucer, *Complete Works*, ed. W. Skeat, Oxford 1903; 'The Nut Brown Maid', *Oxford Book of Ballads*, ed. A. Quiller-Couch, Oxford, 1910, pp. 295–307.

6 La Tour Landry, *Livre pour l'éducation de mes filles*, ed. de Montaiglon, Paris, 1854. English transl. *The Book of the Knight of La Tour Landry*, ed. Thomas Wright, Early English Text Society, 1906.

7 Introduction to *The Miracles of the Blessed Virgin Mary*, ed. E. E. Power, London, 1928. *Miracles de Nostre Dame*, ed. Gaston Paris and Ulysse Robert, Société des Anciens Textes Français, Paris, 1898–1900.

8 *Early English Lyrics*, ed. E. K. Chambers and F. Sidgwick, London, 1947.

9 *Editor's note:* It has recently been argued that the cult of the Virgin was not a cause but a consequence of the higher regard for women in the twelfth and thirteenth centuries: Jacques Le Goff, *La Civilisation de l'Occident Médiéval*, Paris, 1964, pp. 355–6. It has also been suggested that the drain on the knightly class set up by the Crusades helped to enhance the position of women in the upper ranks of society.

10 *Les Troubadours*, ed. R. Lavaud and R. Nells, 2 vols., Paris, 1960–6; J. Anglade, *Les Troubadours*, Paris, 1908; English translation of selected poems in Barbara Smythe, *Trobador Poets*, London, 1911; English translations of selected minnesongs in F. C. Nicholson, *Old German Love Songs*, London, 1907, and J. Bittell, *The Minnesingers*, vol. I, Halle, 1909.

11 *Le Roman de la Rose*, ed. Ernest Langlois, 3 vols., Société des Anciens Textes Français, Paris, 1914–24 (standard edition); *Le Roman de la Rose*, ed. A. Mary, Paris, 1947 (modern French version); an English version in *The Roman of the Rose*, transl. and ed. F. S. Ellis, London, 1900.

12 *Early English Carols*, ed. Richard Leighton Greene, Oxford, 1935, pp. 265–6.

13 Albertus Magnus, *De Bono*, vol. XXVII of his *Opera Omnia*, Aschendorf, 1951.

14 *Oeuvres de Eustache Deschamps*, vol. ix, ed. G. Raynaud, Société des Anciens Textes Français, Paris, 1894; Antoine de la Sale, *The Fifteen Joys of Marriage*, ed. and trans. R. Aldington, London, 1926; idem, *Little John of Saintré*, trans. Irvine Gray, London, 1931; F. Desonay, *Antoine de la Sale aventureux et pedagogue*, Liège, 1940; see also authorities cited in C. S. Lewis, *The Allegory of Love*, Oxford, 1936, pp. 14–17.

15 Geoffrey Chaucer, 'The Legend of Good Women' in *Works of Geoffrey Chaucer*, ed. A. W. Pollard *et al.*, London, 1908, pp. 1581 ff.; Alain Chartier, *Oeuvres*, ed. du Chesne Tourangeau, Paris, 1617; *La Belle Dame sans Merci*, ed. A. Piaget, *Romania*, t. XXX–XXXI, XXXIII–XXXIV, 1901–5; *Le Miroir aux Dames*, ed. A. Piaget, Neufchâtel, 1908 (attribution to Chartier criticised in editor's Introduction).

16 *Medieval English Lyrics*. ed. R. T. Davies, London, 1963, no. 174.

17 'Sententiarum Libri Quatuor' in *Petri Lombardi Opera Omnia*, t. II (Migne. *Patrologia Latina*, Ser. 2, tom. CXCVII, Paris, 1855), lib. II, Dist. xviij: 'De formatione mulieris,' pp. 1046 ff; also pp. 687–9.

CHAPTER 2

1 Thomas Wright, *Womankind in Western Europe*, London, 1869.

2 Johannes Busch, *Liber de Reformatione Monasteriorum*, ed. Karl Grube, Geschichtsquellen der Provinz Sachsen. Halle, 1886, p. 779.

3 John Smyth, *The Lives of the Berkeleys*, ed. Sir John Maclean, London, 1883–5.

4 F. Pollock and F. W. Maitland, *The History of English Law*, vol. ii, 2nd ed., Cambridge, 1968, pp. 390–1.

5 *Wills and Inventories Illustrative of the Northern Counties of England*, part i, Surtees Society Publications, vol. 2, 1835, pp. 68–74.

6 *The Fifty Earliest English Wills*, ed. F. D. Furnivall, Early English Text Society, no. 78, London, 1882, pp. 37–41.

7 *The Paston Letters*, ed. James Gairdner, vols. i–iii, London, 1896. Supplement, London, 1901.

8 J. H. Burton, *History of Scotland*, vol. iii, London, 1867, p. 21. *The Buik of the Croniclis of Scotland*, ed. W. B. Turnbull, Rolls Series, vol. iii, London, 1858, pp. 341–2.

9 Calendars of Patent Rolls, Edw. IV, 1461–7, HMSO, p. 67.

10 D. Oschinsky, *Walter of Henley and other treatises on Estate Management*, Oxford, 1971.

11 *An Abstract of Wills etc. in the Old Diocese of Lincoln*, ed. A. Gibbons, Lincoln, 1888, p. 181.

12 E. E. Power, *The Goodman of Paris*, as in note 5 to chapter 1.

CHAPTER 3

1 K. Bücher, *Die Frauenfrage im Mittelalter*, Tübingen, 1910, pp. 5–7.

2 *Calendar of Plea and Memoranda Rolls of the City of London, 1364–1381*, ed. A. H. Thomas, London, 1929, p. 114.

3 *Issues of the Exchequer*, ed. F. Devon, London, 1837, p. 133; *Calendar of Plea and Memoranda Rolls of the City of London, 1323–1364*, p. 3; *Calendar of Wills in the Court of Husting, London*, ed. R. R. Sharpe, pt. 1, London, 1899, p. 238.

4 *Rotuli Hundredorum tempore Henry III, Edward I*, vol. i, London, 1818, p. 403.

5 Even better known and documented are the cases of widows holding hereditary shrievalties. Cf. Rose Graham, *English Ecclesiastical Studies*, London, 1929, pp. 361–8.

6 *Statutes of the Realm*, vol. ii, p. 158.

7 *Statutes of the Realm*, vol. ii, pp. 57, 338.

8 *Calendar of Plea and Memoranda Rolls of the City of London, 1323–1364*, p. 274.

9 *Ibid.*, *1323–1364*, p. 219.

10 J. Toulmin Smith, *English Gilds*, Early English Text Society, London, 1870, p. 180.

11 *The Great Red Book of Bristol*, ed. E. W. Veale, Bristol Record Society, 1938, part ii, pp. 67–9.

12 *Calendar of Plea and Memoranda Rolls of the City of London*, pp. lix–lxi, 99–102, 107; *Calendar of Letter Books of the City of London*, ed. R. R. Sharpe, London, 1902: vol. D, pp. 51–7, 108–10, 114; also *ibid.*, I, p. 134.

13 *Rolls of Parliament*, vol. V, p. 508 (1463–4).

14 *Le livre des métiers d'Etienne Boileau*, ed. René de Lespinasse and François Bonnardot, Paris, 1879.

15 *The Vision of William Concerning Piers the Plowman by William Langland*, in three parallel texts, ed. W. W. Skeat. 2 vols., Oxford, 1886, p. 51.

16 Bertha H. Putnam, *The Enforcement of the Statutes of Labourers*, Studies in History of Columbia University, vol. XXXII, New York, 1908.

17 *Statutes of the Realm*, vol. II, p. 380.

18 MS: PRO E179/202/72 (West Riding).

19 *Ibid.* 239/174 (Langham in Suffolk), transcribed in E. Powell, *The Rising in East Anglia in 1381*, Cambridge, 1896, p. 108.

20 *Records of the Borough of Nottingham*, ed. W. H. Stevenson, vol. I, London, 1882, p. 270.

21 J. Gower, *Mirour de l'Omme*, ed. J. Skeat, Early English Text Society, 1886.

22 *Wernher der Gartenaere: Meier Helmbrecht*, ed. F. Panzer, 4th ed., Halle, 1924. English transl. C. H. Bell in his *Peasant Life in Old German Epics* (Columbia University Records of Civilisation), New York, 1931.

23 *Hali Meidenhad*, ed. O. Cockayne, Early English Text Society, 1866.

24 See note 15 to this chapter.

25 *Piers Ploughman's Crede*, ed. W. W. Skeat, Early English Text Society, London, 1867, pp. 16–17.

CHAPTER 4

1 *Robert von Blois: Sämmtliche Werke*, ed. J. Ulrich, 3 vols., Berlin, 1889–95; *Jakes d'Amiens*, ed. Gustav Koerting, Leipzig, 1868; a more recent edition of *Art d'amour* in D. Talsma's *Jacques d'Amiens*, Leiden, 1925; Ch. V. Langlois, *La vie en France au moyen âge d'après quelques moralistes du temps*, Paris, 1926; A. Piaget, 'Littérature didactique' in *Histoire de la langue et de la littérature française*, ed. Petit de Tulleville, Paris, t. I, 1896, pp. 162 ff.; Alice A. Hentsch, *De la Littérature didactique du moyen âge*, Cahors, 1903, *passim*.

2 French version of *Flamenca* in *Les Troubadours*, ed. R. Lavaud and R. Nells, 2 vols., Paris, 1960–6. English transl. F. M. Prescott, *Flamenca*, 1933.

3 Philippe de Navarre, *Les Quatre âges de l'homme*, ed. M. de Fréville, Société des Anciens Textes Français, Paris, 1878; F. Barbarino, *Del regimento e costumi di donna*, Collectio di opere inedite, Tomo 26, Bologna, 1875; Ch. V. Langlois, *La vie en France au moyen âge d'après quelques moralistes du temps*, Paris, 1926, pp. 205–40. Alice Hentsch, as in note 1 above, pp. 81–6.

4 E. E. Power, *Medieval English Nunneries*, Cambridge, 1922, p. 263.

5 E. E. Power, *ibid.*

6 E. E. Power, *ibid.*, p. 269, and the article by J. E. G. de Montmorency cited.

7 *The Plumpton Correspondence*, ed. T. Stapleton, Camden Society, 1839, no. 165. *The Stonor Letters and Papers*, ed. C. L. Kingsford, Camden Society Publications. Third Series, XXIX, XXX, London, 1919, no. 120. H. S. Bennett, *The Pastons and their England*, Cambridge, 1922, pp. 82–5.

8 Roger Ascham, *The Scholemaster*, ed. E. Archer, London, 1870, p. 47.

9 Jean Froissart, *L'espinette amoureuse*, ed. A. Fournier, Bibliothèque Française et Romane B.2, Paris, 1963.

10 L. Eckenstein, *Woman under Monasticism*, Cambridge, 1896, pp. 328 ff.

11 *Statutes of the Realm*, 1405–6, pp. 157–8.

12 MS. Public Record Office, *Early Chancery Proceedings*, 290/176.

13 See note 3 to chapter 5.

14 William Beauchamp: *Testamenta Vetusta*, ed. N. H. Nicolas, London, 1826, p. 52; Elisabeth de la Zouche: *An Abstract of Wills in the Old Diocese of Lincoln*, ed. A. Gibbons, Lincoln, 1888, pp. 91–2; Alice Lady West; *The Fifty Earliest English Wills*, ed. F. J. Furnivall, Early English Text Society, no. 78, London, 1882, pp. 4–10; Thomas Cumberworth: A. Gibbons, *ibid.*, pp. 174–5; and *Lincoln Diocesan Documents*, ed. A. Clark, Early English Text Society, pp. 50, 53. Dorothy Gardiner, *English Girlhood at School*, Oxford, 1929, pp. 88–92.

15 *The Acts and Monuments of John Foxe*, ed. Josiah Pratt, vol. III, London, 1877, pp. 588, 594 ff.

16 'Ballade que feit Villon a la requeste de sa mere pour prier Nostre Dame' in *Oeuvres de François Villon*, ed. Paul Lacroix, Paris, 1908, pp. 111–12.

17 *Editor's note:* Trotula herself is not now considered a real person. The name came to be attached to a compilation by one Trottus of Salerno, a male: Dr Singer's essay in *Essays in the History of Medicine presented to Karl Sudhoff*, ed. Charles Singer and Henry Sigerist, Oxford, 1924, p. 129.

The editors of Rashdall's history of the universities omit Rashdall's account of women doctors of Salerno as 'mythical': Hastings Rashdall, *The Universities of Europe in the Middle Ages*, new edition, ed. F. M. Powicke and A. B. Emden, 3 vols., Oxford, 1936, p. 81.

18 *Chartularium Universitatis Parisiensis*, ed. H. Denifle, Paris 1889–97, vol. II, pp. 255–67 contains the record of the proceedings.

19 The verdict against Felicia, *ibid.*, p. 267, also contains an interdiction against other women practising medicine: Margaret of Ypres, Belota the Jewess and Johanna, Conversa. The indictment of Johanna is also recorded in *ibid.*, p. 256.

CHAPTER 5

1 This chapter is wholly based on the author's *Medieval English Nunneries*, Cambridge, 1922, where the relevant sources and authorities are cited. The notes below have been confined to the statements for which the readers might, in

the editor's opinion, desire immediate reference to sources, or for which Eileen Power's footnotes need supplementing.

2 E. E. Power, *Medieval English Nunneries*, pp. 1–3.

3 L. Eckenstein, *Woman under Monasticism*, Cambridge, 1896, pp. 328 ff. A. M. F. Robinson, *The End of the Middle Ages*, London, 1889, pp. 45 ff.; H. O. Taylor, *The Medieval Mind*, London, 1914, vol. I, pp. 479–86; E. Gilliat Smith, *St Claire of Assisi*, London, 1914; *La vie de Ste Douceline*, ed. J. H. Albanès, Marseilles, 1879; E. Renan, *Nouvelles études d'histoire religieuse*, Paris, 1884, pp. 353–96. *Revelations of Divine Love, recorded by Julian, Anchoress of Norwich*, ed. Grace Warrack, 13th ed., London, 1940. For Euphemia of Wherwell see Dom F. A. Gasquet, *English Monastic Life*, London, 1904, pp. 155–8, with quotation from Wherwell Chartulary.

4 G. J. Aungier, *History and Antiquities of Syon*, London, 1840, pp. 405–9.

5 *Myroure of Oure Ladye*, ed. J. H. Blunt, Early English Text Society, 1873; Introduction, pp. xxvi–xxxi; Syon, Cellaress Accounts, MS. Public Record Office, *Ministers Acts* 1307/22; C. T. Flower, 'Obedientiaries Accounts of Glastonbury and other Religious Houses', St Paul's Ecclesiological Society, vol. VII, pt. II, 1912; Dugdale, *Monasticon*, I, pp. 442–5.

6 *Traité de la Clôture des réligieuses*, ed. Jean-Baptiste Thiers, Paris, 1681, pp. 45–9; *Registrum Simonis de Gandavo Episcopi Saresbiriensis*, ed. C. T. Flower, Canterbury and York Society, 1914: pp. 10 ff.

7 *Visitations of Religious Houses in the Diocese of Lincoln*, ed. A. Hamilton Thompson, Lincoln Record Society and Canterbury and York Society, 1915, vol. II, p. 50.

List of illustrations

25 A visit to the bank. From 'De septem vitiis'. Italian, fourteenth century. MS. Add. 27695, fol. 8r. (*British Library Board*)

26 Silk women. From 'Le livre des femmes nobles et renommés', a French translation of Boccacio, fifteenth century. MS. Royal 16GV, fol. 54v. (*British Library Board*)

27 Attending to the wine. MS. Harl. 2838, fol. 37. (*British Library Board*)

28 The fishmonger's shop. 'Une grisaille ornant "Les Chroniques et Conquêtes de Charlemagne".' MS. 9066, fol. 11. (*Bibliothèque Royale, Brussels*)

29 Wool. From the 'Canterbury Psalter', twelfth century. Derived from the French 'Utrecht Psalter', ninth century. MS. Trin. Coll. Camb. R.17.1, fol. 263. (*By permission of the Master and Fellows of Trinity College, Cambridge*)

30 Cooking. German, 1507. (*Mansell Collection*)

31 Women harvesting. Miniatures from 'Der Jungfrauenspiegel'. No. 15326. (*Rheinisches Landesmuseum, Bonn*)

32 Haymaking. 'June' from 'Les Très Riches Heures du Duc de Berry'. Condé Museum. (*Mansell Collection*)

33 By the fire. 'February' from 'Les Très Riches Heures du Duc de Berry'. Condé Museum. (*Photo Giraudon*)

34 A lady at chess. Ivory mirror case. French, fourteenth century. (*Musée du Louvre*)

35 Music-making, 'Allégorie de la Musique'. Miniature by Robinet Testanzl. MS. Fr. 143, fol. 66. (*Bibliothèque Nationale, Paris*)

36 Christine de Pisan. Miniature from 'Works of Christine de Pisan'. French, early fifteenth century. MS. Harl. 4431. (*British Library Board*)

37 Teaching. German schoolmaster's signboard by Hans Holbein the younger. (*Oeffentliche Kunstsammlung, Basel*)

38 Compounding a potion. From Comestor, 'Historia Scholastica', fourteenth century. MS. Reg. 15.D.I. (*British Library Board*)

39 Nuns in the refectory. Poor Clares in the 'Polyptich of the Blessed Umilta' by Pietro Lorenzetti. Florence, fourteenth century. (*Photo Alinari*)

40 Nuns in choir. Miniature of Poor Clares from the 'Psalter of Henry VI'. French, fifteenth century. MS. Cott. Dom. A XVII, fol. 74v. (*British Library Board*)

41 Nunnery officials. Miniature from 'La Sainte Abbaye'. French, c. 1300. MS. Add. 39843, fol. 6v. (*British Library Board*)

42 A nun in her cell. Wood engraving from 'Heavenly Revelations of St Bridget' printed in Nuremberg by Anthony Köberger, sixteenth century, MS. XIV.11. 62, p. 321. (*Cambridge University Library*)

Bibliography

MODERN AUTHORITIES

H. S. Bennett, *The Pastons and their England*, Cambridge, 1922.

K. Bücher, *Die Frauenfrage im Mittelalter*, Tübingen, 1910.

F. Desonay, *Antoine de la Sale, aventureux et pedagogue*, Liège, 1940.

L. Eckenstein, *Woman under Monasticism*, Cambridge, 1896.

Hans Fehr, *Die Rechtsstellung der Frau und der Kinder in den Weistümern*, Jena, 1912.

Dorothy Gardiner, *English Girlhood at School*, London, 1929.

Alice A. Hentsch, *De la Littérature didactique du Moyen Age*, Cahors, 1903.

Ch. V. Langlois, *La vie en France au moyen âge d'après quelques moralistes du temps*, Paris, 1926.

C. S. Lewis, *The Allegory of Love*, Oxford, 1936.

J. Nyss, *Christine de Pisan et ses principales oeuvres*, Brussels, 1914.

Marie-Josèphe Pinet, *Christine de Pisan, 1364–1430*, Paris, 1927.

E. E. Power, *Medieval English Nunneries*, Cambridge, 1922.

E. E. Power, 'The Position of Women', in C. G. Crump and E. F. Jacob (ed.), *The Legacy of the Middle Ages*, Oxford, 1926.

R. Rigaud, *Les idées féministes de Christine de Pisan*, Neufchâtel, 1911.

G. K. Schmelzeisen, *Die Rechtsstellung der Frau in der deutschen Stadtwirtschaft*, Stuttgart, 1935.

Karl Weinhold, *Deutschen Frauen in dem Mittelalter*, 2 vols., 3rd ed., Vienna, 1897.

Thomas Wright, *Womankind in Western Europe*, London, 1869.

CONTEMPORARY SOURCES, MOSTLY LITERARY, AND SECONDARY
AUTHORITIES RELATING TO THEM

J. Anglade, *Les Troubadours*, Paris, 1908.

Roger Ascham, *The Scholemaster*, ed. E. Archer, London, 1870.

F. Barberino, *Del regimento e costumi di donna*, Collectio di opere inedite, Tomo 26, Bologna, 1875.

J. Bédier, *Les Fabliaux*, 5th ed., Paris, 1928.

Robert von Blois: Sämmtliche Werke, ed. J. Ulrich, 3 vols., Berlin, 1889–95.

Alain Chartier, *Oeuvres*, ed. du Chesne Tourangeau, Paris, 1617.

Geoffrey Chaucer, *Canterbury Tales* in *Complete Works*, ed. A. W. Pollard *et al.*, London, 1908.

Geoffrey Chaucer, 'The Legend of Good Women' in *ibid.*

Eustace Deschamps, *Oeuvres*, ed. G. Raynaud, esp. vol. IX, Société des Anciens Textes Français, Paris, 1947.

Flamenca, transl. H. F. M. Prescott, London, 1933.

Jean Froissart, *Espinette amoureuse*, ed. A. Fournier, Paris, 1963.

John Gower, *Mirour de l'Omme*, ed. J. Skeat, Early English Text Society, London, 1886.

Hali Meidenhad, ed. O. Cockayne, Early English Text Society, London, 1866.

William Langland, *The Vision of William concerning Piers the Plowman*, ed. W. W. Skeat, Early English Text Society, 5th ed., Oxford, 1886; also his *Piers Ploughman's Crede*, ed. W. W. Skeat, Early English Text Society, London, 1867.

Le Miroir aux Dames, ed. Arthur Piaget, Neufchâtel, 1908.

Myroure of Oure Ladye, ed. J. H. Blunt, Early English Text Society, Extra Series, 19, London, 1873.

Philippe de Navarre, *Les quatre ages de l'homme*, ed. M. de Fréville, Société des Anciens Textes Français, Paris, 1878.

F. C. Nicholson, *Old German Love Songs*, London, 1907 (transl. of selected minnesongs).

The Paston Letters, ed. James Gairdner, 3 vols., London, 1896.

Christine de Pisan, *Oeuvres Poétiques*, ed. Maurice Roy, Société des Anciens Textes Français, 3 vols., Paris, 1880–95.

The Plumpton Correspondence, ed. T. Stapleton, Camden Society, 1839, no. 165.

E. E. Power (ed.), *The Goodman of Paris*, London, 1928.

E. E. Power (ed.), *The Miracles of the Blessed Virgin Mary*, London, 1928.

D. Talsma, *Jacques d'Amiens*, Leiden, 1925.

Index

Printed by Printforce, United Kingdom, November 2022